Behind Friendly Lines

MEMOIRS OF A US MARINE IN CHILE

MARK McGRAW

LUCIDBOOKS

Behind Friendly Lines
Memoirs of a US Marine in Chile

Copyright © 2019 by Mark McGraw

Published by Lucid Books in Houston, TX
www.LucidBooksPublishing.com

ISBN-10: 1-63296-403-1
ISBN-13: 978-1-63296-403-8
eISBN-10: 1-63296-356-6
eISBN-13: 978-1-63296-356-7

Special Sales: Most Lucid Books titles are available in special quantity discounts. Custom imprinting or excerpting can also be done to fit special needs. Contact Lucid Books at Info@LucidBooksPublishing.com.

To Margaret

Table of Contents

Acknowledgments

My most profound love and thanks to my wife, Margaret; and to my sons, JD and Jackson; who were stellar travel partners on the Chile adventure. *Grazie mille* to my great friend Johnny Wink, who carefully proofread and encouraged me through the process of writing. *Agradecimientos* to Pat Howard and Alan Faille as well as Francisco, Cucky, Fran, and Dani Fierro for hosting us on our return trip to Chile in the summer (your winter) of 2018. Your hospitality was staggeringly generous to us, and the flame of our friendship remains undimmed by the passage of many years and the distance of five thousand miles. Thanks also to Ouachita Baptist University for providing a grant that helped fund that trip. And thanks to Ouachita Baptist University's Department of Communications and Marketing for high-quality photo scanning.

A section of the chapter entitled "The First Mission" first appeared in *The Font – A Literary Journal for Language Teachers* as "The Roundabout Way."

Heading South

Occasionally, when I was young and needed help doing something,
my father would lean in and say in a conspiratorial whisper,
"Let me show you what I learned when I lived with the Seminoles."
It was one of my most intimate memories with my father, or with anyone.

As a Marine captain in the 1990s, sitting in a classroom with two hundred other Marine captains in Quantico, Virginia, I heard a presentation about the training teams that the US Marine Corps was sending to South America as part of the poorly named War on Drugs. The briefer, a lieutenant colonel with the improbable name of Hamlet Hernández, regaled us with tales of training guys in Spanish in small unit tactics while being shot at on rivers in turgid Amazonian jungles. Listening to him talk was like that camera effect in the movies in which the distance between two people seems to collapse—it was as if he were talking to me. If that makes me sound like a warmonger, you don't understand Marines. On one hand, we don't want to become strangers to our families, but on the other, we do want to see a lot more of the world than Quantico or Camp Lejeune.

Even though I already had experienced a couple of deployments to the Far East and had led a Marine Reconnaissance Company in the first Gulf War, I was enraptured by the thought of leading a small team in Latin America. In the timeframe after the 1991 Persian Gulf War, the Marine Corps was settling into a predictable routine that 9/11 would later render quaint. The fact that I didn't speak any Spanish at the time seemed like a minor wrinkle to be ironed out later. A few years later, working at the Camp Lejeune headquarters for all the Marine Corps operational forces on the East Coast, I was given the opportunity to go to Spanish immersion training with the promise that I could lead a Riverine training team in Perú if I could score well enough on the language test.

My unreasonable desire to see action in a second language in South America was seasoned by an internalized narrative that dated back to my junior high social studies project on mountain men.[1] The fact that mountain men could operate independently in the wild, learn other languages, and map out lands unknown to English-speaking civilizations totally captured my imagination. They wore animal skins, could not only survive but also thrive in the wilderness, and understood the Native Americans culturally and linguistically. To me, they were exemplars of the few humans who could fully inhabit the liminal space between races, between nations, between languages, and between the wilderness and civilization in the American West. On some level I always wanted to be like them and, for better or worse, I took that deeply rooted mythology with me when I started working in Latin America in 1998, blissfully unaware of the imperialist baggage and inaccuracy of comparison of that narrative in the context of working in Latin America near the turn of the new millennium. I relished the opportunity to go to Perú, throwing myself headlong into Latin American culture and the Spanish language. I was neither shot, nor shot at, nor was I stricken with dengue fever, nor mauled by wild animals, but I did contract a case of amebiasis so bad that I thought I would set some hemispheric record for time spent sitting on the toilet. And the Peruvians with whom I worked did not live in grass huts. My running mate was the highly educated and refined Carlos Garrido, a national hero[2] whose English was much, much better than my Spanish at the time.

Back from Perú in 1998, I returned to my alma mater, Texas A&M, to serve as the Marine Officer Instructor under the Naval ROTC program.

---

1. Although they were long dead and not part of popular culture by the 1970s, I studied the histories of Jim Bridger, Kit Carson, and Hugh Glass, and I regarded them as heroes the same way kids look up to pro athletes.

2. At the height of Sendero Luminoso terrorist activity in Perú in the late '80s, Garrido, a Peruvian Navy SEAL, was ambushed by gunmen on his front porch while he was trying to balance a bag of groceries in one hand and dig his apartment keys out of his pocket with the other. He not only survived the attack, but managed to get his pistol out and wound one of the assailants and kill the other.

While at A&M, I audited Spanish classes in the hopes of maintaining my hard-gained Spanish language skills. In the middle of that three-year assignment, I was offered a post in Chile, where I would work as part of an exchange with the Chilean Marine Corps. I was to be assigned to the operations section of their largest unit and employed pretty much as if I were another Chilean officer. The Chileans sent one of their guys to serve with the 5th Marine Regiment in Camp Pendleton, California, as the other side of the exchange. The Chile job would give me the unique opportunity to work and live in another country with my family. Our boys, JD and Jackson, were seven and three years old at the time. I was the only one in the family who spoke any Spanish. My wife, Margaret, was as gringa as McDonalds, and she was initially not at all happy about the assignment. She was comfortable in her home state of Texas, a two-hour drive from her parents, and I was proposing we plunge ourselves into cultural, linguistic, and climatological discomfort on the other side of the world. Her point of view was reinforced when we met the British pastor's wife at our church in Chile. She and Margaret chatted a little and when Margaret told her she didn't speak Spanish yet, she confessed, "Me neither, really." The pastor's wife looked at me and narrowed her eyes before adding, "These men. They drag us everywhere."

Traveling to Santiago, Chile, from the States involves flying all night. If you are fortunate enough to be seated on the left side of the plane, you are treated to a view of the snow-capped Andes colored by the orange-hued rising sun. Since you probably slept poorly, if at all, you could be forgiven for suspecting that you were still asleep, or inhabiting some surreal alternative space, and in a sense, you are inhabiting somewhere surreal. For us, the temperature swing added to the shock of entering a new world. It was 102 degrees Fahrenheit on that July day when we departed the small airport at College Station, Texas, for Santiago, Chile. When we landed in Santiago after flying all night, it was 32 degrees. Margaret frantically dug into her suitcase right there at baggage claim to switch sandals for shoes and socks. Rich Werschel,[3] my predecessor in the exchange officer job, picked us up

---

3. Rich died of a heart attack while working out at a Camp Lejeune gym just days after coming home from a year-long deployment to the Middle East in support of Operation Iraqi Freedom. He was loved and respected by the Chilean Marines.

at the airport and drove us the hour and twenty minutes to Viña del Mar, where we were to live for the next two years.

Within the next couple of days, Rich and I put on our forest-green Alpha uniforms and went down to the *destacamento* for me to report in. ("Destacamento" means "detachment," which in the military context could be a group of any number of people or weapons systems organized for a specific mission.) I met briefly with the comandante, Capitán de Navío Walter Wunderlich. Walter Wunderlich was impressively well-read and had a biting sense of humor. He had small hands and a large face and when he got aggravated about something, his Spanish took on a choppy Prussian quality. His father, Pablo, was nationally famous for commanding the Chilean Marines in the '70s during a border crisis with Argentina.

After meeting with Wunderlich, we went to the *cámara de oficiales* (wardroom) to meet the officers. The wardroom was a large space with a dining area, a bar, and space for large events. It was connected to the Bachelor Officer Quarters. It was clean and tastefully but simply appointed. The thing that made the biggest impression on me was the fact that each officer who entered the wardroom while we were waiting to start came right up to me and confidently introduced himself. I was reminded of the concept of shared space that is so strong in the Spanish-speaking world. Someone who has grown up in Latin America doesn't just stride into a place like they own it. There's always a consciousness of who else is in the space and who may be older or socially senior to you. If you know them, you greet them and speak to them. If you don't know them, you go over and introduce yourself. Once everyone had a glass of wine or pisco sour in his hand, the comandante made a few welcoming comments and toasted. I, having been coached on the importance of reciprocity, returned the toast. As I spoke, I was so nervous that when I patted Rich on the shoulder, I hit him so hard that I made him spill half his pisco sour. But my Spanish wasn't too bad, and the general feeling I got from my new comrades in arms was something like, "This guy's going to be okay."

Threats Real and Imagined

When you go overseas as a US Marine, the threat of terrorism looms largest among the concerns about your well-being. Bad things can happen to anyone anywhere, but for an active duty military person to be attacked by terrorists on foreign soil has an outsized political impact and always will. The summer before we moved to Chile, I asked to be sent through extensive anti-terrorism training. Looking back now, I should have known good and well that Chile was not a high- or even medium-threat country for terrorism. I probably just wanted to do the training because I thought it was cool. And it was.

The first course I attended was HRP—the High Risk Personnel course in Quantico, Virginia, run by Marines for Marines. HRP focused on combat marksmanship with the Beretta 9-millimeter pistol. The majority of our training consisted of quick-draw shooting at a steel torso silhouette target from seven yards away, which may seem preposterously close, but FBI studies had determined that most gunfights involving a pistol take place at that distance or closer. So, combat pistol marksmanship doesn't concede a shooter the luxury of calmly unholstering the pistol, taking the safety off, and carefully aiming at the target. Even at seven yards, under the stress of trying to shoot as quickly as possible, when you had to get the flap of your holster off, pull the pistol, get both hands on it while sweeping the safety off with your thumb, aim, and press the trigger, it turned out there was an awful lot of air around that target where the round seemed content to go. The instructors would stand just behind us and time us with an electronic device that would beep, signaling the start of the shooting process. The device would automatically stop timing when it sensed the noise of the bullet thwacking against the steel target. Although I nearly always scored expert (the highest level) at the conventional pistol range, I was never as fast and accurate as the quickest three or four Marines in the class. The instructors, Marine Corps NCOs and staff NCOs (noncommissioned officers), did everything they could to ramp up the stress, including screaming, "Shoot him!" in your ear as you struggled to draw your pistol. In a class before us, some of the instructors would go and actually stand next to the targets while their students shot, demonstrating that the twin wells of bravery and foolishness in a US Marine are of limitless depth.

We also worked on pistol retention drills and shooting a target that you are actually holding with your non-shooting hand, since studies have shown that a lot of guys who draw their pistols (cops in nearly all cases) wind up getting shot with their own gun in a struggle. One of the most exciting things we did was a shooting competition, having two of us shoot parallel series of steel targets as quickly as we could. The targets were set to fall down after two or three shots (a good training feature since a determined attacker won't be immediately stopped with one shot unless it's between the running lights), and the stress of competition while shooting had a totally different effect on accuracy. For the course's graduation exercise, we swapped out our pistol components for those that would allow us to shoot paintball bullets and went to Hogan's Alley at the FBI Academy to do scenario-based gunfights against the instructors. The HRP course got me much better at combat pistol marksmanship, but also convinced me that being accurate and fast in a real gunfight from a cold start (especially if you're carrying a concealed pistol) is a very difficult thing. The week after HRP in Quantico I went to a course called Sudden Violence at a non-military training facility in Northern Virginia.

Sudden Violence was one of a series of courses run by retired and former Marines and cops. For most of the training day, we'd learn to fight from a position that was most probable in a scenario where you're being ambushed. Ever since the days when we humans were trying not to become dinosaur food, we will, when threatened, hunch our head and shoulders down, throw our hands (open hands, not fists) and arms up, drop our center of gravity down a little, and square ourselves up on whatever's threatening us. In this course we also learned how to fight unarmed against clubs and knives and handguns, the overarching lesson of which was to avoid a fight at all costs. We mostly practiced strikes and kicks against pads and sometimes on each other, and we fairly crawled out of there sore, bruised, and bleeding when the course ended.

We also got briefings on safely traveling overseas and staying in hotels, getting through roadblocks, and picking up on indicators of impending attacks. The best general advice I took away from those classes was that as a totally military-looking North American, I have no chance of blending in, but I can do my best to look like I belong. So, don't walk around in a place where you may be under a threat while looking at a cell phone or at a map. Walk like you know where you're going and have a purpose for going there. And always assume you're being surveilled, that every keystroke in an e-mail is being read, and every word said on a phone is being recorded. We watched a lot of video, not of conventional military situations, but of holdups in convenience stores, street shootouts between law enforcement and suspects, assaults of pedestrians, and scenes that some of the instructors had videoed while working on security details overseas. My suspicions about the efficacy of pistol gunfights were confirmed in many of the videos of real gunfights, usually filmed by police cruiser dashboard cameras. They were frantic, imprecise, wild-firing engagements at short range in which shooters would sometimes fail to hit their adversaries with a single shot on target, and even if they did, would rarely finish the fight with a single wound. The gunfights often wound up as wrestling matches, even if one or both combatants had been shot multiple times.

The next week I attended an anti-terrorism driving course at a racetrack in West Virginia. My classmates and I were lodged at a hotel in Virginia and drove rental cars to and from training every day. At the track, we were issued helmets (an ominous sign, I thought) and put into car teams consisting of three students and an instructor. We received a little classroom orientation before being told that there was Dramamine available to us for motion sickness and that the medicine was a preventative, not a remedy. I remember rolling my eyes at that measure, thinking it was a little extreme, but was convinced otherwise soon after we got into the car. Our instructor, a big, sloppy guy who was an amateur racecar driver, took us out for our first lesson on braking. The idea was to brake just hard enough to avoid skidding. We learned to listen for the telltale chirping sound that tires would make just before too much brake pressure caused them to lock up. We were soon getting up to eighty miles an hour before braking as quickly as we could and would often wind up skidding. By the end of the day the tires had so many flat places on them, I had the sensation of driving a Flintstones car with lumpy rocks for wheels. The tires would be replaced most days. We drove retired police cars, Caprice Classics, and spent much of the driving time at eighty to one hundred miles an hour when we weren't trying to negotiate a turn as quickly as possible without sliding off the track into the hay bales. In spite of my volunteering for airborne school and parachute duty, I'm not a big high-speed thrill seeker. I won't bungee jump, I don't particularly enjoy roller coasters, and I was never that guy who sees how fast he can get his car to drive on an empty highway late at night. So, after each driving session I would get out of the car somewhat wobbly-legged and nauseated.

Not only did we drive on a wet skid pad and practice driving the car in a controlled skid, we learned how to use the parking brake to lock the back wheels and skid into a 180-degree turn. We learned the bootlegger turn where you jam the car into reverse, get up to about thirty-five miles per hour, brake into a skid while turning the steering wheel, then snatch the car into drive to speed away. We not only learned in theory, but we actually practiced running through roadblocks formed by other cars. The engine makes the front of the car heavier, so if you can ram into the side of the roadblock car at the rear axle, even at twenty miles per hour, it will spin out of the way and allow you space to drive through. I was never any better than average at the techniques of high-speed driving. I drove my best on the night tests, when the only things to focus on were your own technique and the sliver of road your headlights illuminated at any moment.

Not all the training took place behind the wheel. We shot up a recently-junked car with shotguns, pistols, and rifles to see what it would take to make the gas tank explode. Not even tracer bullets that illuminate in flight will set the car on fire, even with the tank two-thirds full of gas. Now that you know that, when you're watching a movie and a car gets shot up and explodes into a ball of fire, you can lean over and whisper to the person watching it with you, "I know for a fact that doesn't happen."

At the end of each day at the track, we would drive back to our hotels some twenty miles distant. The training so desensitized me to speed that I'd catch myself driving ninety-five on the interstate without realizing it. Slowing down to sixty or sixty-five felt as if I were driving a riding lawn mower. At the hotel after the track training, we'd have classes, going over case studies on terrorist attacks and gleaning lessons learned. At that time, Greece was still a country rated high-risk for terrorism. There was some group in Athens that specifically targeted US military personnel and seemed to take great pleasure in shooting guys with an old US-issued .45-caliber pistol they had stolen years before. That group also did car bombings, and one of the best stories we heard was based on the confession and debriefing of a captured terrorist who had been part of a cell tasked with rigging one of the official US vehicles in Athens with a car bomb. The terrorists could never figure out a good time and place to rig the car because the American driver was an especially hard target when they surveilled him. Every morning before he left for work, he carefully checked around the vehicle, opening the trunk and checking under the hood. When the US interrogators congratulated the "hard target" for his vigilance, he explained that the car leaked oil so badly that he had to put a quart of oil in the engine crankcase just about every morning before driving it, and he carried around a case of oil cans in the trunk just to ensure a steady supply. The embassy motor pool's slow response to his repeated requests to have the car repaired may have saved his life.

We learned to plan our routes, to vary them as much as possible, and to look closely for chokepoints where we had to slow down or stop. Those were the places and times that called for maximum vigilance. It's common that we heighten people's awareness to the risk of terrorism during pre-deployment training, but when we send them somewhere without teaching them how to intelligently scale that awareness up and down, they get off the plane and stay on high alert over the first three or four days. Then, worn out from hyper-vigilance, they stop varying routes and times of travel, checking vehicles, and sticking to a buddy plan.

For my first day of work at the destacamento in Chile, my sponsor told me to wear my camouflage utility uniform[1] and wait at the busy corner a couple of blocks from my temporary house for a pickup at 7:15. Almost without exception, married officers in Chile have one car in the family and Mama drives it. We officers who worked at Fuerte Aguayo hired a van to come by our homes and pick us up before work and then take us back home from the base at 5:30 p.m.

I obediently waited for the van at the corner in my camouflage utility uniform with my black backpack slung over my shoulder. As I stood there waiting, with traffic whipping by, the driver of one of the cars that slung around the corner took a flash photo of me out of the driver's side window. My heart started racing as I watched the car zoom north toward Valparaíso. Here I was on the first hour of the first day in uniform in Chile and I was being surveilled, however clumsily. I didn't get a great look at the driver, but I was 90 percent sure it was a man and he had absolutely, purposely taken a photo of me as he drove around the corner. This episode perfectly reflected the case studies I had been taught wherein terrorists always do extensive surveillance and planning before committing an attack. I was certain that the events had just been set into motion for a terrorist attack. After a nervous first day at work, I went to the Naval Section Chief's house and reported to him what had happened. I also made a report to the US Military Group at the embassy in Santiago.

For good reason, a lot has been written about the abuses of the Pinochet regime during the '70s and '80s, but not many people in the States know that there were many acts of terrorism against the military in Chile during those years. The Manuel Rodríguez Patriotic Front, known by their initials in Spanish FPMR, remained active in Chile even after the return of democracy, and their targets included gringos and, strangely, Latter-day Saints churches. In 1990, the FPMR rigged a bomb in a softball bat that killed a Canadian and injured a US embassy officer, giving the FPMR points for creativity among terrorists in addition to a successful cowardly attack. Jack Stradley, a guy who had been the exchange officer a few years before me,

---

1. In the Marine Corps, we called these cammies. In the Army, they're called BDUs (Battle Dress Uniform).

told me before I deployed to Chile that the FPMR had nailed a threatening note on his garage door.

This photo incident, then, had me very concerned until a few days later when I found out who the photographer was: a Chilean Navy officer on his way to work in Valparaíso who saw me and decided to capture proof of me breaking the Chilean Navy uniform policy. It turned out that the Chilean Navy, of which the Chilean Marines are a specialty (not a separate branch of the military like the US Marines), had recently strictly prohibited the wearing of cammies outside of military bases and training areas. The only uniform Marines could legally wear out in town (including commuting to and from work) was the Navy dress blue uniform (the equivalent for me was the green Alpha uniform). I don't know if we hadn't gotten the word yet or if we were just slow in complying, but by standing out on the corner in cammies waiting to be picked up for my first day of work, I was unwittingly violating the policy. If it is not obvious by now, Chilean Navy guys don't like Chilean Marines any more than US Navy guys like US Marines. The Chilean Marines, like their US counterparts, embrace and celebrate their distinctiveness. Chilean Marines refer to themselves unofficially as *cosacos* (Cossacks), appropriating the folkloric iconography of a Slavic warrior class. A key difference between US and Chilean Marines, though, is that in Chile, the Marines are actually part of the Navy, so discrimination can have real traction in the form of penalizing guys, in seemingly infinite ways, for opting to be Marines instead of ship drivers. A lot of Chileans are as European-looking as most US Marines, so I strongly doubt that the photographer was singling me out as a US Marine. Our camouflage utility uniforms are nearly exactly like those the Chilean Marines wear. So this was not a Chile versus US thing, but a Navy versus Marine thing.

We were still living out of our suitcases in a temporary house in Viña del Mar when, on the morning of August 1 at about 5 a.m., our older son, JD, came into our bedroom to wake us up. He calmly told us his brother's pillow was on fire. By the time we could get to the boys' bedroom, Jackson's bedding, mattress, and carpet were also ablaze. The fire had produced a thick column of toxic black smoke that hung near the ceiling above the upper bunk bed. Margaret pulled Jackson off the burning mattress and headed for the back door. My first thought, "I got this," quickly changed when I tried to pull the burning mattress off the bed and wrestle it out of the house. I suppose that moving the mattress just supplied the fire with more oxygen, because I had the sensation of the flames growing and wrapping around me, burning my hands and making me drop the mattress. Within mere minutes—and it may have even been seconds—we gave up on trying to fight the fire from inside the house and got out. The only thing we saved besides our children was an already-outdated IBM Thinkpad laptop that we used to e-mail back to the States via the finicky dial-up internet.

August in Chile is the middle of winter—dropping into the forties at night—and we had been trying to keep the boys' room warm with a little electric heater that came with the house. During the night, Jackson's pillow had fallen off the bed and come in contact with the heater, catching fire. The fire investigators later told us that, in most cases, a fire in a carpeted room with bunk beds will kill the child in the upper bunk, not from the flames of the fire itself but from the toxic smoke produced by carpet, mattresses, and bedding. But JD providentially woke up in time to climb out of that bed, save himself, his brother, and possibly, all of us.

Back when I was starting to learn Spanish, it didn't occur to me that I'd someday have to use it to stand in the street and yell for help at the top of my lungs, but that was all I could do since we couldn't go back into the house and didn't have cell phones. And as the light of day started to spread over Viña, we made a pretty pitiful sight huddled in the driveway of the house next door, red-eyed, our faces smeared with soot, snot, and tears, our eyelashes melted into curly-cues by our contact with the flames. Later, as I watched the firefighters finally coming out of the house high-fiving each other, I thought to myself, "Well, you wanted an international adventure for your family. You got it."

Carreta

Francisco and Cucky Fierro were a great help to us after the fire. It made perfect sense that the Armada would assign Francisco to be my sponsor. He was a Capitán de Corbeta, the Navy rank equivalent to mine; he and Cucky spoke English well; and he had just returned from the flip side of the exchange: two years with 5th Marine Regiment in Camp Pendleton, California. Francisco is a friendly, personable guy who needs to shave twice a day. He's the son of a naval officer, which was very common in Chile, but Francisco's dad, Pedro, had long since left active duty, having been connected to one of the worst disasters in Chilean naval history. In 1965 Pedro Fierro was the captain of the Leucotón, a tugboat that was maintaining lighthouses along the notoriously tempestuous southern coast when they were forced to take refuge from a storm. The storm broke the anchor chain and the ship ran aground. The Janequeo, a larger tug, came to free the beached Leucotón. The tow line got tangled in the propeller of the Janequeo, which was then battered against the rocky shore by enormous storm-generated waves. The Janequeo broke in two, and fifty-one men were killed. Although he was not personally at fault for the disaster, Francisco's father resigned his Navy commission the next day. The rusted hull of the Leucotón is still encrusted in the beach at Purranque. In his post-Navy life, Francisco's dad ran a construction company that went bankrupt along with many other businesses during the general economic disruption of Salvador Allende's first couple of years as president of Chile. About the time Francisco's father went into full financial collapse, Francisco entered the Escuela Naval, Chile's Naval Academy. He was fifteen years old.

Figure 1: With Capitán de Corbeta Francisco Fierro at Destacamento Miller, Fuerte Aguayo near Concón, Chile, in August, 2000

Francisco and I would be sharing an office at Destacamento Miller. He was the operations officer and I was to be his assistant ops officer as well as the training officer for the unit. Maybe due to his Basque[1] ancestry, Francisco is a much bigger guy than the average Chilean. His default setting is happy, and it is difficult for me to picture him or think of him without also remembering his laugh. He may have learned or inherited his cheerful nature from his mother, whom he addressed with the formal *usted*. She was so nice, it was thought that if she were to unwrap the gift of a single old shoe on Christmas morning, she would smile broadly and pronounce it the finest shoe she ever received. Cucky (pronounced "cookie") Fierro's real name is Marcela. It seems that no woman in Chile goes by her given

---

1. Nearly half of immigrants to Chile in the 1600s and 1700s came from Basque country, the ethnically and linguistically different region of northern Spain. To this day, to have Basque ancestry is fundamental to being a *cuico*, claiming a place in the upper echelons of the unofficial Chilean caste system.

name, which can create a lot of confusion for outsiders. Some nicknames are obvious. Nearly every Cecilia is Chi-chi, and many nicknames are simply a mashup of the woman's first and middle names. Carmen Gloria, for example, goes by Calo. And then there's the ubiquitous María. Some are María José or María Jesús. María Irene will wind up being called just Irene and María Esther will just be Esther. Cucky is petite and attractive and goes about the business of being a wife and a mother as if she is delivering fire to mankind. She calls Francisco "Gordo" (Fatty), a common term of endearment that Latin American wives inflict on their husbands. They have two beautiful kids, Francisco (Franciquito) and Daniela, who are a little older than our boys. Franciquito was such a hard-core fan of the Chilean national soccer team when we lived there that he would have to be separated from the TV when they were losing. The Fierros spent a lot of time with us and showed us around much of Viña. One of my best memories was going with the Fierros to a seaside restaurant in Concón called Las Deliciosas. It was a real informal place, kind of a no-frills café, with white plastic chairs. You went there to eat empanadas, and that's it. The nearly ubiquitous empanadas of Latin America were known as meat pies in Natchitoches, Louisiana, where I first had them, but in Chile they're something special and considered an element of national patrimony. At Las Deliciosas there were empanadas with cheese, with different types of seafood, and what must be considered the national food of Chile: empanadas de pino with ground beef, boiled egg, and pine nuts. In the middle of our meal, a street musician came in with a guitar and sang "Puerto Montt," a '70s Chilean pop music standard. When the guitarist got to the chorus, Francisco belted it out *a todo pulmón* (as loud as he could).

The school year, the work year, and the calendar year in Chile are all synchronized. You're on summer vacation in January and you start in your next school grade or your new work assignment in February. When I started work at the destacamento and JD started school in July, it was right in the middle of the annual cycle in Chile, so I worked closely with Francisco for only six months before he changed jobs and moved away. They were six critical months because he helped me through the timeframe where, paradoxically, as a new arrival I needed to accomplish the most and was the least equipped with knowledge of language and systems. In addition to sharing an office, we shared a room in the Bachelor Officer Quarters, just a place to store our uniforms and gear and a place to sleep if we were ever to be restricted to the base for some reason. For my first six months in Chile, Francisco was my *carreta*. "Carreta" literally means "cart," but in the Chilean Navy your carreta was your running mate, your best friend, the guy who could be counted on to come and bail you out of hard times and personal disasters. Guys in the Chilean Navy and Marines even affectionately addressed each other as carreta. Your carreta would generally be someone from your class at the Escuela Naval. Although the carreta relationship was typically symbiotic, Francisco was not my carreta because I could do anything for him, but rather, he was my carreta for what he could do for me.

Soon after starting work at the destacamento, all the officers had to take the semiannual physical fitness test that included pull-ups, a shuttle run, a rope climb, sit-ups, and a four-mile run. At least on paper, the pull-ups on the Chilean Marine test were supposed to be scored pretty much like the ones we did on the US Marine Corps physical fitness test. To get credit for a complete pull-up, your chin had to get above the bar, and then you had to come all the way back down and extend your arms. Thankfully, you were not required to pause at the top or bottom of the repetition. Pull-ups were an important event because they were worth five points each, for a total of one hundred points if you could get twenty. Since even hanging on to the bar costs you energy, it is important to do them rapidly, but not so quickly that your muscles seize up. I trained for pull-ups pretty regularly, and like a lot of Marines I could usually get twenty, even after the US Marine Corps outlawed "kipping" in the late '90s.[2] To get to twenty, though, I would generally have to do sixteen without stopping, and then gather myself before grinding out the final four repetitions with a couple of big breaths between each one.

So, when we started the fitness test that day at the pull-up bars behind the enlisted barracks at the destacamento, I did my pull-ups and then took

---

2. "Kipping" is generating momentum by swinging the lower body. Go to any crossfit gym and you'll see it being used. I knew guys who were not particularly strong in the upper body who could easily get twenty pull-ups just by mastering the gymnastics of this technique.

my place as the counter for the guy next in line, who turned out to be Francisco. He jumped up, grabbed the bar, and started cranking away on his pull-ups, but when he would get to the top of his range of motion, his chin would remain a good six inches below the bar, not even close to a legal pull-up. I counted out loud, "cero, cero, cero." After about four frantic failed repetitions, he stopped and looked at me incredulously, his body hanging from the bar like a sack of potatoes, his face red between his extended arms. I could sense a wave of discomfort among the officers queued up behind the pull-up bars. Francisco was one of the more senior guys in the unit and my de facto carreta, and here I was not counting his pull-ups in front of all the other officers. He eventually dropped off the bar and I explained to him that he wasn't getting his chin high enough, which he took with stoic resolve. He rested for a while and eventually got back up and did enough legitimate pull-ups to pass that part of the test. It hurt his score, though, and made him look bad, and I was too ignorant to feel as remorseful about it then as I do now. Looking back through the rearview mirror of experience, as his carreta I would have been expected to credit him with a pull-up about every time he could minimally bend his arms.[3] If the comandante or segundo comandante had seen it, either of them might have jumped in and said, "Hey, those don't count," but at least we would have been admonished together, which would have been more important than any test score. One thing I didn't realize at the time but figured out eventually: no officer junior to Francisco and me would have said squat about me giving him credit for crappy pull-ups.[4] Luckily for me, Francisco had just been with the US Marines for two years and I think he knew that we were generally a little more *cuadrados*, literally "square" or inflexible when it came to enforcing the rules. If he ever held a grudge, it never showed.

Like many other things in Chile, it took some time for me to learn how serious the carreta relationship was, but from very early in our relationship I was conscious of and thankful for all that the Fierros did for us. A common

---

3. This kind of "brother-in-law'ing" was not unique to the Chilean Marines. I occasionally saw it done in one form or another in US Marine aviation units and reserve units.

4. Another Chilean Marine with whom I served, Yayo Aranda, once told me there's a reason why Chilean military headgear has a visor: so that you look down, or straight ahead, and never up.

Chilean saying is "It's better to have friends than money," and I believed it. I still believe it. Our friendship with the Fierros even changed how I talked. Before I ever went to Chile, when I was at Quantico or Camp Lejeune, the phrase "He's a great American" was in fashion among Marines. We would use it to describe someone who was a good guy, a mensch. But to us, the term "American" only applied to people from the United States.[5] To most US Marines who have never been challenged to expand their definition of the word "American," Francisco wouldn't be one because he is Chilean. So I stopped using that phrase. Francisco Fierro is a great human being, which must be a more admirable, rare, and remarkable thing.

---

5. Latin Americans and Canadians are also "Americans," so the most accurate term for us in describing our nationality is "North Americans" or *norteamericanos* or *estadounidenses* in Spanish.

The First Mission

After the fire in the temporary house, my family and I lived in the Mykonos hotel for nearly three weeks. It was a nice hotel with a kind of seaside resort feel to it, but it was about three miles out of town down the coast from Viña toward Concón. We started shelling out about sixty-five dollars per day on the credit card to stay there. From our balcony we could hear the surf crashing against the rocky shore, and a lot of the time we could see seals play on the rocks just off the beach. But other than that, and ping-pong, there was nothing else to do, and since it was the middle of winter, there were few other guests. We were also still jittery from the fire in our last house. I would lie awake and hear the woosh of the gas coming on in the heater when the temperature dropped until I'd eventually drop off into fitful sleep. We had a feeling of being stranded out there since we had no car (our van that we shipped from the US hadn't arrived yet[1]) and the bus only came by at unpredictable times about once an hour. We had to hire a taxi (more money spent every day—cash this time) to take JD to Mackay School, and I would sit down in the lobby with him to wait for us to be picked up.

Most mornings, when we would sit in the lobby, a well-dressed, middle-aged woman would come into the lobby of the hotel. She'd have on high heels and makeup, and her hair was nicely done. I assumed she was the

---

1. When it finally got through customs and arrived to us, our Toyota Sienna van made quite a splash in Chile. It had an automatic side door and full-time running lights, which prompted some people to stop us when we drove in the daytime to inform us that our lights were on. Our friends called it "la van de la NASA." Chileans seemed to consider the National Aeronautics and Space Administration to be the world's foremost producer of new technology. Most anything high-tech, new, and unfamiliar might be called "de la NASA."

business manager of the hotel or some events coordinator. She would greet the desk clerk and us with the manners of a century gone by before disappearing into a room in the back. I always had the odd sensation that I had seen her somewhere else, though, and some time near the end of our three weeks at the hotel I figured out that she was the lady who cleaned our room. The little closet in the back was where she would change out of her power suit into her uniform and comfortable shoes, wipe off her lipstick, and get to work. That was a pattern I was to see for the two years we were there: Chileans will dress as nicely as they can to travel to and from work, even if it's for a half hour, get into their work clothes, work all day, and then reverse the process for the trip home. It may have been their way of saying, "I may clean other people's toilets all day, but I'm not going to look like it when I don't have to." It could also be interpreted as an attempt to guard oneself against the classism that would make people look down on a hotel maid, or some combination of those two (or a dozen more) factors. I doubt she ever subjected the custom to much analysis. Chileans generally dress about as well as they possibly can and take care of their personal appearance. One of the worst insults from one Chilean to another seems to be *te ves picante* (you look nasty), which refers to one's dress and grooming.

Once we got JD's school transportation figured out, it was time to find a place to live. We looked at several places and finally settled on a nice home to rent in Viña del Mar. That accomplished, we had to wait for the place to be approved by the US embassy in Santiago.

Since we were waiting, I went back to work at the destacamento. Rich Werschel had warned me not to come to work at the destacamento until my family was all settled. "Once you show your face down there and start working," he said, "they're going to want you involved in everything, every day, all the time."[2] Since it looked like it would be at least two weeks until

---

2. The destacamento took seriously the idea that I was there to be employed just like any other Chilean officer. Occasionally, US officials from the embassy would forget that and I'd get a cell phone call from the US Military Group at the embassy in Santiago asking me to come escort some visiting official from the States. The first time it happened, I told Comandante Wunderlich, and he responded with something like, "Well, I better get a letter from them, because you work for me." He was exactly right. One of the goals of an exchange program is to foster mutual respect and understanding, but you send the wrong message if you don't bother to ask the host nation's military commander if you can borrow the guy you've assigned to him.

we could finalize our rental agreement and move into a house, I went into work. They were chomping at the bit for me to get back to the destacamento because August was a busy training month and they had planned a deployment for the whole unit to the south of Chile. The training year had a lot of little deployments with company-sized units out to the local training areas. There were also opportunities for company-sized units to be trucked to places a few hours away, but the opportunities to board the amphibious ships with the whole destacamento and sail several days away, either to the cold, rainy south or the warmer desert north to train for a few weeks were expensive, rare, and, therefore, important. On this mission, I was designated to go with a task force under the command of Jorge Budge, a guy the same rank as me. If Budge doesn't sound Spanish, that's because it's not; it's Scottish. That's the case with a fair number of Chileans, a country of immigrants like many others. The fact that Valparaíso was a coaling station for ships sailing around Cape Horn and up along the west coast of South America brought the Brits for over a hundred years. Budge, our task force, and I boarded a small amphibious ship, the *Chacabuco*, and sailed south from Valparaíso (the rest of the unit was aboard other ships). Budge, Francisco Fierro, and the other officers were enthused to show me the famously cold and rainy south of Chile, and I wanted to go on the mission in spite of the fact that much of my personal military gear was still in shipment from the States (I went on this deployment wearing jungle boots and carrying a cheap sleeping bag I got at a sporting goods store in Viña). I was enormously bothered by the fact that I was leaving Margaret in that hotel without transportation and without much to do. Since she couldn't speak Spanish, she didn't even feel comfortable trying to board a bus to get around town. While I was deployed, I had no way of communicating with her, either, to give her tips on what to do. We were all still in shock from the fire. Bills were piling up and we were close to maxing out our credit cards. We paid the hotel bills weekly. I'd ride the bus into town and fax the receipts, along with a request for reimbursement, to the US Marine Forces South administration office in Miami. Then we'd wait for the next month's pay cycle to come around and hope they entered all our reimbursable expenses. I still had no cell phone at that point (you had to have the equivalent of a Social Security number to get one, and we still had not been assigned one by the Chilean government), so I was sending in these expenses in the blind, hoping they'd get from the fax machine to the correct clerk. I couldn't justify not going on the mission since we were on hold to get our home approved, so I tied up all the loose ends I could and left for what was to be a two-week deployment.

Winter meant rough seas, and I started to feel queasy soon after we sailed from Valpo. I've never been too prone to seasickness (a guy I deployed with once to the Western Pacific went to bed when we crossed under the Coronado Bridge in San Diego and didn't get vertical until we got to Okinawa), but I'm not totally immune to it, either. I've usually found that if I can get above decks and see the horizon, I can function. There was little for me to do but sit in the officers' mess, a space about as big as a living room, and read. I read up on doctrine, manuals, and regulations of the Chilean Marine Corps and Navy. And I felt isolated because my Spanish wasn't strong enough to fully participate and socialize. For reasons I couldn't fully appreciate, I was struggling to comprehend Chilean Spanish.

I came to learn Spanish in a roundabout way. I never took a language in high school and, curiously, I was not required to study language as part of my undergraduate degree in geography. The semester I was to graduate from college, I was annoyed to discover that I was required to take at least one three-hour language class to fulfil the requirements of my Naval ROTC scholarship. I went directly to Rick McPherson, the Marine colonel who ran the program, and begged him to waive the required language class. "I'm going to be fighting people, not talking to them," I reasoned.[3] Satisfied to remove a potential stumbling block between me—a mediocre student—and graduation, he waived the requirement.

But the presentation on training teams in Latin America that I heard ten years later infected me like a virus and I resolved to start teaching myself Spanish . . . someday. A year later, before deploying on ship to the Mediterranean for six months, I got a couple of cassette tapes from the Defense Language Institute (DLI). I'm sure DLI produced many valuable language learning tapes, but the ones I came across consisted entirely of words in Spanish

---

3. No one is more unshakably certain about the specifics of his or her future than a college senior.

followed by the equivalent word in English with a pause between. The words were entirely random. *Flecha* . . . arrow . . . *vaca* . . . cow . . . *habichuela verde* . . . green bean. It was a dreadful way to try to learn Spanish, but there I'd be at 6 a.m., in the ship's gym pedaling away on the Lifecycle listening through the headphones of my Walkman and whispering the answers to myself. I even made flashcards I could study when I couldn't have the Walkman with me. I remember being confused about how *bondadoso* is defined as "kind," with no way to know if it was "kind" like "Be kind to animals" or "What kind of dog is that?" When I got back to Camp Lejeune and it looked like I might get a chance to go to immersion training in Guatemala, I started working with a CD-based Spanish program for an hour or two early in the mornings before work. It would teach you phrases you'd need on a trip, one chapter about the airport, another about the hotel, and so forth. It included written and oral comprehension of words and short phrases and even graded phrases for pronunciation that you spoke into a microphone. I learned, for instance, that the phrase, *No te preocupes* meant "Don't worry." I didn't know that it was a command, or that it was reflexive, or whether you said that to one person or a group of people, or whether you might be a little unduly familiar saying that to a person much older or senior in rank to you.

When I went to Guatemala, then, I was armed with a few phrases of introduction which I could pronounce smoothly and rapidly. I arrived in Guatemala City and was transported by a Guatemalan driver from the US Military Group to Antigua a couple of hours away. He valiantly tried to teach me a few words along the way. I remember him replicating with his hand the motion of driving up a steep incline while saying slowly, "Subir, subir." When we arrived at the Francisco Marroquín Language Project,[4] I was met by a couple of staff members and my first instructor, all of whom spoke only Spanish. They warmly welcomed me and seemed delighted that I could deliver a few smooth, well-pronounced greetings. They started to engage me in polite conversation and, my working knowledge and comprehension

---

4. Proyecto Lingüístico Francisco Marroquín was the biggest and seemingly most reputable of what seemed to be a hundred Spanish schools in Antigua. The school taught Spanish to foreigners and used the profits to study, document, and preserve indigenous languages in Guatemala.

of Spanish exhausted, I smiled uncomfortably and shook my head. I punctuated my linguistic poverty with an open-hands gesture you would use to say, "That's it. I have no more money." Confusion spread across their faces and one of them asked the driver something that sounded like, "Well, can this guy speak Spanish or not?" The body language and tone of his response seemed to say, "Oh, this guy can speak all kinds of Spanish." Of course, it took them just a few more seconds to confirm that I knew basically nothing. Downcast, one of them handed me an information folder with the name and address of my host family along with a map and instructions for where to show up for class the next day. Since I had never had a language class, I was colossally ignorant and incurious about language learning methodology. I believed that I'd just sit across the table from a Guatemalan person and we would simply speak and listen to each other, and eventually I'd collect enough words and phrases to be conversant. I had no idea that I would be tasked with systematically rewiring my brain with a different logic from the one I had inhabited for thirty-four years.[5]

Classes at the language project were one-on-one. The students and teachers sat across from one another at little wooden tables separated by stacks of butcher paper upon which the instructors would write upside down. The tables were arrayed around the courtyard of a home. My first teacher was Irma Floridalma, who went by Flory. She was less than five feet tall, with short, shiny black hair. So strong was her indigenous heritage that she looked Asian. She was always impeccably dressed, highly capable, and all business. I soon saw that the methodology was to be within the grammatical system, which intimidated me since I was never a confident grammarian in English. We started with regular verbs in the present tense, and she showed me how the suffixes shifted according to a pattern that corresponded to the subject pronouns, just like you would do with a twelve-year-old. She would write out and explain the pattern in a way that I somehow comprehended and ask me, "¿Entiendes?" (Do you understand)? "Sí," I would respond. "Bueno," she would say. "Vamos a practicar" (Let's practice). She would then run drills at me with the aid of a textbook that looked like it had come over with the

---

5. Spanish is a Romance language. English is a Germanic one. Although there are many Latin-based cognates, they obey different systems of logic.

conquistadors, verb after verb, subject pronoun after subject pronoun until I couldn't do any more, the way you would imagine a boxing trainer would oblige a fighter to hit the heavy bag until the fighter was unable to lift his hands. "Next, these verbs are irregular in the present. You must memorize them, Marcos. ¿Entiendes? Vamos a practicar."[6]

Other than a short lunch, we'd break for only a few minutes for machine-brewed, real, fantastically strong coffee, which was unusual in Antigua. The coffee grown in the fincas that covered much of the volcanic hillsides surrounding the town was for export, and the Guatemalans who lived in Antigua mostly drank freeze-dried. Flory would never work with me at a pace at which I was comfortable, a concept known in language pedagogy as "+1."[7] We were always pressing forward into the immense universe of what I didn't know. I was way beyond the ideal age for language learning. My brain had already lost much of the plasticity required to rapidly learn new things. The synthetic nature of the verbs, the way the subject pronoun would disappear because it was implied by the form of the verb mystified me. The syntactical difference of putting the object pronouns before conjugated verbs never failed to confuse me as to who was doing what to whom. I felt the urgency, too, to learn everything I possibly could in my seven-week stay. I was to take the Foreign Service Institute (FSI) exam at the end of the course and then the Defense Language Proficiency Test (DLPT) when I got back to Camp Lejeune. Then there was the practical concern of going to work in Spanish with guys carrying weapons and live ammo in Perú, where there would be a bounty on me and my teammates.

I lived with a Guatemalan couple and their three kids. María and Hugo made a living by running a tiny convenience store out of the front of their home and keeping students. At any given time, there were three to five other students from Europe and the US living in the house. The family

---

6. If this sounds like the dreaded "drill and kill" method disparaged by so many non-traditional language programs, it is. But we also learned an enormous amount of language through exposure to a high volume of comprehensible input, learning to understand (and later mimic) what our instructors were telling us as they roamed into unfamiliar grammar and vocabulary. Somehow (I attribute it more to the instructors' skill than mine) I nearly always understood everything my instructors told me although it was always in Spanish.

7. +1 means that the student is always straining to add just one more concept, one new grammatical or syntactic wrinkle. But +2 is too much, the student becomes humiliated, frustrated, and defeated.

spoke only Spanish and enforced the rule of "only Spanish at the kitchen table," but we students spoke English among ourselves. The other students tended to be college-aged, so I usually spent most of my weekends alone. I felt like an idiot trying to speak Spanish to people in the restaurants and shops. The highlight of most weekends was a fifteen-minute call home on a pay phone adjacent to a crowded restaurant.

A few other military guys also attended the school. In the interest of keeping a low profile, we wore civilian clothes and grew our hair out a little bit. When the US military sends people abroad, the primary concern is terrorism, but petty crime was infinitely more probable in and around Antigua, with tourists occasionally being robbed at knifepoint in broad daylight. One day, when Flory and I talked about the difficulty for military guys to truly blend in with the civilian gringos attending the school, she said, "We know exactly who you guys are. Look at that guy over there, his shoes, the way he sits. Of course, he's military." She was right. Still, when other students asked me why I was studying Spanish, I'd answer, "I have always wanted to read Cervantes in the original language," a foolish answer since I only had a vague idea that Cervantes wrote *Don Quixote* and couldn't tell you any more about the book than an average high schooler could.[8]

New language learners generally make rapid progress and hit occasional plateaus, and I was no exception. I spent two weeks run aground on the famous preterit/imperfect problem, the two basic past tenses. The instructors were not allowed to speak English, and all Flory could do was repeat the list of rules for when to use each tense. I eventually worked through all the indicative mood (present, preterit, imperfect, future, conditional, present perfect, past perfect) while mixing in object pronouns, adjectives, adverbs, and numbers. The instructors were required to correct every single error we made, which prevented me from having anything like a fluid conversation during a lesson. The interruptions particularly annoyed me when I talked about my family, whom I missed terribly. One day about four weeks in, my teacher and I went to the coffee machine and he let me talk for about five minutes without stopping and correcting me. I knew what I said wasn't

---

8. Sixteen years later I would write my doctoral dissertation on *Don Quixote*.

mistake-free, but he let me stumble and stagger through a couple of subjects and verbal tenses as he asked me questions and prompted me with comments. I walked away from that moment realizing that I had just become a Spanish speaker in the same way we become swimmers when we discover the ability to submerge and propel ourselves through the water a short distance while holding our breath. During my final week in Antigua I had a few days to explore the subjunctive mood, which to me was like some kind of cruel trick.[9] At that point, I had so much grammar clanging around in the attic of my brain I couldn't manage any better than a vague conceptual grasp of it. I scored a disappointing 2 on the FSI exam (with 3 being the highest) on my last day of school. On my last night at Hugo and María's, *The Simpsons* dubbed in Spanish was playing on the small TV in the kitchen. Of course, the mouths didn't match the words that were spoken in goofy cartoon voices, but I was sorely disappointed that I could understand almost nothing of the dialogue.

When I got back to the States, though, a couple of Marines who were Spanish speakers told me I had picked up an impressive amount of Spanish in that short time and was doing well. I took the DLPT and got a 2 in listening and a 3 in reading (3 was the highest. A score of 2/2 was good enough to deploy to a Spanish-speaking country). I bought better cassette tapes, some produced by Pimsleur and others made by Berlitz, and wore them out listening to them. My nearly six-month mission to Perú was a fabulous learning experience, and I'd study the subjunctive at night after the training day had ended. During my two years working at Texas A&M, I audited intermediate and advanced Spanish classes taught by some superb lecturers. Before I left Texas A&M to move to Chile, I took the DLPT again and scored 3/3.

When people ask me the best way to learn Spanish, whether the preferred method is through taking a grammar class, listening to music, watching

---

9. It was as if the conjugations I had worked to learn for the previous six weeks were a fool's errand. The subjunctive is a grammatical mood we rarely use in English but is used all the time in Spanish. I didn't realize that forming the subjunctive was very similar to the process of making formal commands: flipping the thematic vowel from "a" to "e" and "e" or "i" to "a" while watching out for a handful of irregulars. Trying to teach me subjunctive my last week in the course was like handing a brick to a drowning man.

telenovelas, watching movies with subtitles, reading the newspaper, or talking to native speakers, I say yes. All contact with the language is good. All exposure to the new language helps you ingrain and internalize it, even the crappy vocabulary tapes I started with. The reason people don't retain most of what they learn in a high school or college grammar class is not because it's poor instruction, but because a single exposure is usually not enough for retention. For me, it took several doses and several applications of Spanish, with a little time for the "paint to dry" between each coat. I'd be taught an idiomatic expression or grammatical construction in a lesson in Guatemala or a classroom at Texas A&M; but later I'd overhear someone else using it in context; then a month later I'd hear it in a song; then I'd read it somewhere. At some point it would come out of my mouth for the first time, probably incorrectly. A few repetitions later, I could say it correctly, eventually fluidly and without thinking. Then I'd have it.

But here I was, finally plunged into the contextualized language environment of the Chilean Navy, and I was embarrassed and frustrated by how poorly I was doing. I struggled through some of the most basic conversations with some of the Chilean officers, leaving them with looks on their faces like, "Get a load of this guy." My disappointment was compounded by the fact that I was doing poorly in something I considered myself pretty good at. Even though a lot of the officers spoke some English, I was doggedly determined to speak nothing but Spanish with the Chileans. I knew that it would only take an overheard spare phrase in English here and there for rumors like "He can't speak Spanish" and "He only wants to speak English" to start spreading. And I didn't want a crutch. I trusted that the sooner I bashed through the discomfort of poor communication skills, the better the whole experience would be.

Since adult learners of a second language store their new language in a different part of the brain than their primary language, it could be argued that you are something of a different person when you speak your second language. I believe this phenomenon could certainly describe me. I'm not normally an especially outgoing person, but in Spanish I'll talk with the taxi driver, the yard man, or anyone else who seems the least bit disposed to conversation. A stray conversation here and there constitutes a great learning opportunity: about the language, local geography, customs, systems, and values. And certainly, it's an attempt to earn the ego-stroking compliment by the other person for speaking their language well.

There are several reasons why Chilean Spanish is especially difficult to comprehend. The first goes back to the original Spanish conquest and settlement of the Americas beginning in the 1500s, when conquistadors and colonists came over from Andalusia and Basque country, the extreme southern and northern parts of Spain. Being from the extreme periphery of Spain, the Spanish of those settlers was not as conventional as the Castilian spoken by people from Spain's geographic and political center. To pronounce *leche* as "leshe" and *chico* as "shico" (which Chileans consider a sign of unsophistication and poor education) is a linguistic echo of the time before the 1500s in Spain when Castilian Spanish in the south of Spain was still heavily influenced by Arabic. Another reason for the uniqueness of Chilean Spanish is that, because of Chile's geographical isolation on the extreme edge of South America, words unique to Chile have developed that are different from what a North American or European will learn in a Spanish class (*polola* instead of *novia* for girlfriend, *choclo* instead of *maíz* for corn, *palta* instead of *aguacate* for avocado, *poroto* instead of *frijol* or *habichuela* for bean, *mina* instead of *mujer* for woman, *gallo* instead of *hombre* for man, *fome* instead of *aburrido* for boring). The third phenomenon is a Chile-specific second person familiar (*tú*) form of address (a *voseo* considerably different from either the peninsular Spanish or the rioplatense spoken on the other side of the Andes). To top it off, spoken Chilean Spanish is lightning fast, and some of the "s's" and "d's" disappear from the middles and ends of words. I confess that I love the sound of Chilean Spanish. Many dialects of Spanish are musical, but Chileans, especially those from Santiago, employ an unusually high tone to emphasize a point and punctuate sentences with the word *po*, which would be *pues* everywhere else in the Spanish-speaking world. Today, years after leaving Chile, I can still identify a Chilean just by hearing a couple of phrases. Riding the city bus in Florence, Italy, in 2016, I overheard two twentysomething guys speaking Spanish. I guessed that they were not only Chileans, but from Santiago. I staggered from handhold to handhold across the rocking bus to them and struck up a conversation to confirm my guess. I was correct.

Regarding the comprehension problem, in my defense I must point out that something in the national DNA causes Chileans to often answer direct questions with responses that have nothing to do with the question asked. If they feared that an accurate answer to a question I posed might reveal a lack of knowledge or diligence on their part, they would simply respond with information they wanted me to know. For example, I would ask a soldado on a field training exercise a question like, "Why do you have the mortar set up here?" He might answer, "Bueno, mi mayor, lo que pasa es que[10] (Well, Major, what's happening is) . . . the sun came up from over here . . . and the wind was blowing from over here . . . and we never got breakfast this morning." During my first few months in Chile I would walk away from an exchange like that shaking my head, crestfallen at what I took for my poor comprehension. "I thought I understood all the words he said, but it didn't make any sense so I must be wrong." Eventually, if it were in a work context, I would listen patiently to the response without interrupting, and then say, "Magnífico, pero mi pregunta fue . . . (That's great, but my question was . . .").

In addition to pure linguistic challenges and the national idiosyncrasies about answering uncomfortable questions, I would also run into comprehension problems which were rooted in simple systematic differences. Paying for groceries was an exercise in confusion and frustration until I figured out the system. Early in our time in Chile I'd pay for groceries with a credit card (Visa seems to be universally accepted in Chile), something that should be laughably easy and straightforward, but I would run into problems. The checker will run the card and first ask you, "¿Con cuotas o sin cuotas?" I had never in my language learning run into the word "cuotas"[11] and since it's a false cognate with the English word "quotas," I became mired in the quicksand of incomprehension. Even if you had a good dictionary at hand (and the grocery store checkout line is not a good

---

10. This phrase was usually employed to give the speaker time to invent an adequately believable response.

11. I have taught college Spanish with at least four different textbooks, and I don't think I've come across "cuotas" in the basic vocabulary, either.

place to pull that out), "cuotas" in the way it's being used here is third or fourth down the list of possible English definitions. The first definition is actually "fees." Do you want fees? No, I don't want fees. But it's not "fees" in the Chilean checkout line. What they are asking is if you want to pay for your purchase in monthly installments, a possibility I never considered since I'm generally always paying my credit card expenses in installments anyway. In Chile you may also be asked at the cash register if you want to donate the change that would round up to the next peso to some charity. Hogar de Cristo (Christ's Home) was common. But the checker, in a hurry, bored from saying the same thing all day, and probably looking at the cash register while he or she says it, says something that comes out as a stream of unintelligible utterance ending in –isto. So you say yes. Or no. Or you ask for clarification with a line of people waiting behind you. She or he explains. You still don't understand, so you say no just to be safe. The cashier frowns because either you didn't understand or were too stingy to give something like sixty-three centavos (equivalent to about ten cents in US currency) to help poor people. You shuffle out with your groceries confused and embarrassed with what you're sure are the stares of twenty Chilean people burning holes in your back. It would often occur to me that people visiting the US would run into similar systematic mismatches that went beyond language, resulting in the same confusion and embarrassment for them in my country. But I confess that I would often get angry and frustrated in Chile. I had been to language training, after all. I had classes. I had passed a test. I was the only member of my family who spoke Spanish when we first got there, so it seemed like there was a lot riding on my capability, but fundamentally I was too proud a person to gracefully handle being a little embarrassed and I would often act like a jerk. Sometimes a little jerk. Sometimes a big one. I'm sure I was not a fun guy to be around on that first deployment to the south.

After sailing for a couple of days, we pulled into Puerto Cisnes, a picturesque little fishing village at the edge of Chilean Patagonia. As the ships refitted, I stood on the pier with Francisco Fierro and Comandante Wunderlich. I confessed to Wunderlich that I didn't understand much of what was going on, and even less of what was being said over the ship's intercom. "I'm not sure if the ship is on fire or if it's time for lunch," I said. "Don't worry," he responded with the sarcasm that I would come to like about him when it wasn't directed at me. "Just watch the sailors. If they're walking, the ship is on fire. If they're running, it's time for chow."

It was in Puerto Cisnes where we got the ship stuck on the beach during a practice amphibious offload. For most ships, running aground is the worst thing imaginable, but these ships were made to beach themselves headfirst, open a clamshell-type arrangement in the front of the ship that allowed a ramp to come down, and offload rolling stock and Marines afoot on shore. We beached on the narrow rocky shore at Puerto Cisnes just to offload and reload a few vehicles, and when the tide came back in, it didn't come in high enough to immediately float the ship again. At one point we got all the Marines aboard to stand on the fantail of the ship where there was a little helicopter landing pad. We even jumped up and down in a futile attempt to wiggle the front end of the ship off the beach. As we jumped, Jorge Budge and I looked at each other and laughed and started singing a colossally stupid song by King Africa that was popular in the discos at the time, "Saltando sin parar" (Jumping without end). It didn't work and we had to wait another eight hours or so until a higher tide lifted us off the beach.

As we sailed south along the coastline, we would occasionally get into range of TV stations and have enough signal to check out the news or a soap opera. I was able to glean that Chile would play Brazil in a soccer match the first night we'd be ashore on our mission. A *subteniente* in our unit turned to me and said, "No hay ninguna posibilidad" (There's not any possibility), referring to Chile's chances of winning against perennial powerhouse Brazil in soccer. We'd also pass cell phone towers, and the sudden availability of a signal prompted the officers to gather on the fantail, pull out their cell phones, and call to check on things at home. I was initially confused by the proliferation of cell phones since I was sure that I heard and understood that they were strictly prohibited on a deployment. I eventually figured out that if something is strictly prohibited but impossible to control, everyone does it, just not in front of the comandante.

Figure 2: Zodiac rubber boats on the deck of the Chilean Navy amphibious ship Chacabuco.

Our navigation took us through the Golfo de Penas, which would be rendered into English as the Gulf of Sorrows, a notoriously rough section of water that seems to live up to its name for the easily seasick. It turns out, though, that the original name for the gulf was Peñas, probably for the first Spaniard to chart or sail the area. English charts couldn't replicate the "ñ" and the mistake turned out to be adopted as truth since the water was always so rough there. The mission for our task force was to do a reconnaissance of the isthmus of Ofqui that connects the Taitao Peninsula with the mainland. The ship went as far south down the canals as the icy, progressively shallower water would allow, and we eventually craned several outboard-engine-powered Zodiac rubber boats over the side of the ship and then clambered down nets to board them. The hours we spent getting to and traversing Laguna San Rafael were incredible. Ice-chest-sized chunks of ice became Volkswagen-sized and then small-house-sized chunks through which we navigated. I was in a boat with six or seven Chilean Marines and none of us besides the coxswain had anything to do but look around for obstacles.

During the transit a corporal fished out of his jacket a chocolate bar (bought, not issued). He opened it and broke off a piece for everyone in the boat. He was left with the same sized square as everyone else got. This got my attention because US Marines don't share like that. As a US Marine I may let a buddy or two have a dip of my Copenhagen, but it's my can of snuff; I bought it, and I'm keeping just about all of it for myself. I saw the same Chilean process of sharing, wherein the owner of the goodies completely distributed what he had, whether it be chocolate, peanuts, or coffee, replicated several times on this and other missions with the Chilean Marines. We eventually dragged the boats ashore on a rocky beach adjacent to the spectacular San Rafael glacier. I was exhilarated as we set up our bivouac, wondering if I was the first North American or even English speaker to set foot on that remote place. We huddled around campfires that night and listened to the soccer game on our radios. I soon got bored and sleepy and crawled into my sleeping bag in the tent I was sharing with Jorge Budge. No sooner did I get in the bag than I heard cheers and shouts of "¡Gol de Chile!" echoing up and down the beach. The good guys eventually scored two more goals and wound up winning 3–0 in a game that didn't count for much besides national pride.

The next morning, we suited up in wetsuit bottoms and GORE-TEX jackets to traverse the isthmus and reach the bay on the other side. We were to cross what was essentially a semi-frozen swamp. Starting down a faint trail that ran from the back of the beach where we bivouacked, I looked up and saw, nailed to a tree, a wooden sign with the words from Dante's *Inferno* neatly engraved *in English*, "Abandon all hope, ye who enter here" (so much for my foolish fantasy of being the first gringo to set foot in there). In most of the places, there was not enough water to run the boats, certainly not with the outboard engines engaged, but the ground wasn't dry, either, so we had to carry the boats a few hundred yards at a time through three inches, or six inches, or a foot of water to a place where the water was deep enough to run the boats. An empty Zodiac boat is not a big deal for eight Marines to carry, but with gear, fuel bladders, and a 55-horsepower engine, wading through mud and water under a day-long intermittent drizzling cold rain for what amounted to miles was totally exhausting. We eventually got through to the San Tadeo River that communicated with the Pacific, loaded into the boats and motored to the ocean, took photos and GPS fixes, and reversed the entire process. Since we had burned off some outboard engine fuel, we were a little lighter going back, and returned cold, tired, and hungry just before dark.

With the mission accomplished, we bivvied in the same spot as the night before. There was no soccer game being played, so the night was silent except for the sounds of the glacier "calving," heaving off enormous chunks of ice into the lake. There would be an otherworldly groan of ice moving, then cracking, then splashing into the water. I was tired, but happy that I had had so many great experiences on my first deployment with my Chilean unit. I was happy and relieved, too, that in a few days I'd be home to take the next steps to normalcy for Margaret and the boys. On the navigation back north toward home, we made a port visit to the island of Chiloe, a unique part of Chile with fascinating old wooden churches and its own folklore, a fusion of indigenous practices and Jesuit-sponsored Catholicism. We wandered around town in civilian clothes, did a little shopping, and went to a restaurant for dinner. While we were there, we got a message that a fishing vessel was lost at sea, and our ship was tasked to assist in the search and rescue efforts. The rest of the destacamento sailed home on the other two ships and we stayed behind. Budge, the bachelor, was ecstatic. It was an opportunity for him to do something operational in command of a task force, a chance for recognition and experience for him. Budge was happy for another reason: he was able to board a helicopter for a short search and rescue flight around the archipelago east of Chiloe, which entitled him to a month of flight pay. For me, it was a few more days away from home, which I admit I was not happy about. I had to try to put a good face on and not complain, though. The Marine Corps, whether the Chilean one or the US one, is not Burger King. You can't always have it your way.

The fishing vessel wound up being found without our efforts, and we sailed from Chiloe for home just a day later than planned. The last night aboard culminated with a party in the officers' mess conceived by Budge and the ship's captain. Budge wanted Mexican food. The captain wanted karaoke. The resulting party featured some approximations of Mexican food heavy on lettuce, pisco sours, and a Chinese karaoke machine loaded with American songs that were almost exclusively John Denver hits (with English and Chinese printed lyrics). We sang "Country Roads" in English a todo pulmón.

A New Home and a Shipwreck

We searched for a house to rent and eventually found a fine home in Viña del Mar owned by a retired Chilean admiral. It had the look of a Swiss chalet on a steep hillside in a neighborhood called Jardín del Mar. We'd be fairly close to Mackay School and just a couple of blocks from the home of the US Naval section chief where we'd go to pick up our mail. But it wasn't as simple as just signing a rental agreement and moving in. We had to get a security specialist from the US embassy in Santiago to come out to inspect the house and approve it. After a few scheduling missteps, we were able to meet her at the house for the inspection. This house's yard, like most yards in that neighborhood, had a high fence around the property that included a metal gate that slid back and forth on a rail. Our big metal gate was not motorized and required someone to get out and slide it open to drive in and out of the garage (a perfect job for a seven-year-old boy). The inspector looked at me like, "You poor, stupid man," and said, "This gate doesn't open automatically. Can you picture yourself having to get out and manually push this heavy gate open every day?" Since at that point our family had been living out of our suitcases in a temporary house and hotel, riding the bus and carrying laundry and groceries up and down the steep hill from the bus stop for weeks, I said something like, "Lady, I'm *dreaming* about pushing this gate open every day."

The house passed inspection and we started the process of renting it. The property manager was Silvia, the sister-in-law of the owner, a realtor who worked out of her home a few blocks away. I would have to make an appointment to see her. Her housekeeper would let me in and seat me in the living room, and I would wait up to fifteen minutes for the señora to come in. I would guess she was in her seventies, with a regal air and blonde wig. She wore a back brace that encompassed just about her entire torso. Meeting with her was a requirement for renting the house, although I don't remember anything we talked about. I eventually met with another lady from the real estate agency, who supervised me while I walked around the house and filled out an inspection sheet (in Spanish, of course) that ran to eight pages. In Chile the custom is to take all your appliances with you when you move out, and some of our appliances wouldn't work in Chile, so we wound up having to buy just about everything down to the light fixtures. We set up our family laptop in the office and got the internet working. It was still dial-up for us and everyone we knew in Chile from 2000–2002. Broadband internet access (*banda ancha* in Spanish) was still one of those nice improvements that was a few years away. Sometimes we'd work up an e-mail to the folks or friends back home and hit Send, and then ten days later find that it was still sitting in the "out" box as a draft. That would happen when connection was lost while the computer was in the process of trying to send the e-mail.

One thing we did make work was our own refrigerator, which required a transformer the size of a small bowling ball to step down the electricity for such a big appliance from 220 to 110. We had to pay a month's rent in advance in addition to another month's rent as a security deposit, which ran to about $6,000 that we had to put on our credit card. Initially, to pay the rent I would have to ask for the morning off from work, take two buses to a bank in downtown Valparaíso where I would withdraw enough cash to bring back to Viña. Eventually, we opened a checking account and I was able to just write and drop off checks at Silvia's. No checks or important correspondence was ever to be mailed, since the national postal system was not trusted by the homeowners or the real estate company.

We moved into the house in mid-August and essentially camped in it until our household goods got through customs just before the end of the month. I literally climbed over boxes of our newly delivered household goods on my birthday to leave the house for a twenty-day training deployment to Iquique, the northernmost big city in Chile. As cold and rainy as Viña is in the southern hemisphere winter, Iquique is dry, dusty, and graffiti-infested. The first night I was there I went out with Jorge Budge and a couple of other officers, including the medical officer, Andrés Llarena. Andrés was a big, friendly guy who had lived in Oakland, California, when he was little. He spoke English well and, despite claiming to have been traumatized by having to stand up and pledge allegiance to the flag of the United States every day in junior high, we became fast friends. We had a few hours to kill before we had to go back to the ship, so we went to dinner and then to a movie at the local mall. The film we saw that night was *Taxi para tres*, a Chilean film that had won some awards that year at a Spanish film festival. It may have been the first non-Hollywood movie I had ever seen and I was struck by how average the actors looked. Of course, I knew none of the actors and had a terrible time understanding the dialogue, which bothered me until I read an article about the film that pointed out that when *Taxi para tres* was shown at a film festival in Spain, it required subtitles in Spanish.

Before the unit training in Iquique started, Jorge Budge wanted to take me out for a run that I understood him to describe as "not too far" and at "a relaxed pace." We left the ship in the afternoon and started out down sidewalks through neighborhoods at a brisk trot. I was in pretty good running shape but the pace was uncomfortably fast for me. From that moment to this there has never been any doubt that ours was not to be just a collegial, friendly run. As is the custom of Marines just about everywhere, it was "run to the death" as each of us was trying to get the other to drop or to slow down or stop. We went up and down short sand dunes, crossed beaches, and ran down by the waterline, through industrial zones and past dusty, vacant lots before finally turning back for home. I suffered mightily but did my best to feign a relaxed jog. We never slackened the pace as our shadows lengthened that afternoon. We never stopped for water, either, and eventually made it back to the ship at almost sundown after what I later estimated to be a twelve-mile run in the late-day heat of the coastal desert. Like fighters who embrace after a brutal fight that goes to a decision, we slapped hands and agreed that the run had put a serious hurt on us both as we caught our breath and cooled down walking around the pier.

Part of the training exercise in Iquique was a joint amphibious exercise with a task force from the US called UNITAS. The landing force for UNITAS was a reinforced Marine rifle company, who embarked aboard one of the smaller amphibious ships for a four-month lap around South America as a means of showing the flag and building interoperability with the navies of countries like Venezuela, Brazil, Argentina, Chile, Perú, and Colombia. We (the Chilean and US Marines) were to do an amphibious landing near a desert training area in the north of Chile, capped off by a live fire exercise against static targets. We exchanged some units. A platoon of US Marines and a section of 81-millimeter mortars came aboard our ship along with some amphibious assault vehicles. The Chileans were enthusiastic about going ashore in the AAVs since it meant a ride into mock battle in an unusual vehicle and the chance to arrive on the beach with dry feet, which is never assured when you do the assault in rubber boats, as the Chileans routinely do. Budge and I were to come ashore together in one of the AAVs, while Andrés Llarena, the medical officer, was to travel in one of the rubber boats. Andrés, who was senior to Budge, was indignant. He confronted Budge in mock belligerence, pointed at him threateningly, and asked, "Why do I, who am senior to you, have to start the exercise with my trasero mojado (wet butt) and you get to start the exercise with trasero seco (dry butt)?"

Our side of the landing went off without a hitch, but we never saw the other part of the landing force arrive from the US ship, the USS *La Moure County*. We soon found out that in the predawn maneuvers to land the AAVs and rubber boats, the US ship did the unthinkable and unpardonable: it hit the rocky shoreline and ripped a long hole in its hull. They immediately did damage control, sealed off the flooded compartments and kept the ship afloat, but they were done for the day. In fact, already an old ship relegated to the Navy Reserve, that ship never operated again. It was towed to the shipyard at Talcahuano, stripped of its electronics, and eventually intentionally sunk off the coast of Concepción, some 932 miles south of where she suffered her mishap. When I overheard Chileans asking what happened, the answer was something along the lines of "woman driver." A US Navy female lieutenant had control of the ship's bridge when it ran ashore, which baffles me to this day. Why would you have such a junior officer, of either gender, driving the ship at such a dangerous and critical time? The incident seemed to only confirm the Chileans' suspicions that they were right to resist further integration of their navy along gender lines as they saw the US Navy doing. The assumption that women are worse drivers is even codified in a politically incorrect popular saying, "Mujer al volante, peligro constante" (If there is a woman at the steering wheel, there is constant danger).

Budge and I spent a long time during the exercise watching the US Marine 81-millimeter mortar section firing at targets along the ridgeline at the edge of the training area. Budge was delighted by how responsive and accurate they were. Mortars, like artillery, are an area weapon. You put the first round out there hoping to get near the target and then adjust the next one or two, but our guys were often getting within effective range of the target on the first shot. "¡Seco!" Budge would exclaim over and over. *Seco* means "dry," but in that context it was like "Dead center!" or "Bull's-eye!"

After the exercise, the literally shipwrecked US Marines were bussed to our destacamento near Concón, where they lived and trained for a couple of weeks in late September 2000, until a new ship came to embark them. While they lived at the destacamento with us, Budge was responsible to Comandante Wunderlich for them, which seemed to be a constant source of anger and frustration for Budge. When weapons cleaning was on the schedule, he would go down there and see that some of them were smoking cigarettes while they were cleaning their weapons, which was prohibited in the Chilean Marines. In the Chilean Marines, you don't smoke until it's time for everybody to smoke and some officer tells you it's okay to smoke. Budge couldn't communicate his displeasure in English so he'd come vent to me. I responded that I didn't see a problem as long as the weapons got clean. Eventually, Budge told me he thought the US Marines were undisciplined and lax, which angered me. The passage of many years and the translation from Spanish to English prevent me from telling you what I said with absolute accuracy, but it went something like, "Oh, really, Jorge? Undisciplined? What was it you were saying while we watched the US Marine mortars firing? What did you say over and over? Seco. That's right. You remember. Seco. We're disciplined about the things that are important." That was the end of the discussion.

In Which La Gringa Alta de la Tierra Lejana Stars

I imagine it would be excruciating to be an introvert in Chile. Life there is incredibly social. There are always dinners and parties and cookouts and receptions and celebrations to attend. And you must attend. Even dropping your kid off to spend a couple of hours with a classmate whose family you know well requires that you also go in the house, have coffee and something to eat, and chat for at least twenty minutes. Being busy is never an excuse for not socializing. There always seemed to be family activities and activities for adults, but not a lot of specific, structured activities for kids besides school and birthday parties. I never knew of any youth soccer leagues or kids being taken to piano or dance lessons in Chile. When adults had social activities, they would almost always bring the kids, who would entertain themselves or be supervised by an older child until it was time to go home. Chileans have a saying that goes something like, "If you're planning to go somewhere that you don't want to take your kids, you may want to reconsider if you should be there yourself."

One year we were invited to participate in an event sponsored by the British expats in Valparaíso to celebrate St. Andrew's Day. The celebration involved lots of traditional Scottish dances,[1] which necessitated several weeks of practice on Wednesday nights. We'd all meet at a school gym somewhere in Viña, put a cassette tape in, and attempt to learn our dance steps while the kids played in the corner of the gym. The whole arrangement seemed to me

---

1. North Americans learning Scottish dance taught by British expats while speaking Spanish in Chile rivals my Chinese karaoke Mexican dinner experience earlier in my Chile tour in terms of maximum internationality.

to be supremely healthy. The kids saw that mom and dad had something going on that was for them, and that they as kids had the responsibility to stay out of the way and keep themselves busy for a while.

A Saturday bike ride I went on with the commandant of the Chilean Marine Corps and some other Chilean Marine officers took about five hours, which included only about two hours of actually riding the bike. Of course, it wasn't the bike ride that mattered as much as spending time together, conversing, listening, laughing, and relaxing on the patio behind the officers' club at the midpoint of the ride. For a senior officer to invite me to participate in that off-duty activity was a gesture of intimacy and confidence as well as a test of how well I'd socialize. Those experiences built bonds of understanding and solidarity, and they were vital to my ability to form friendships with my Chilean counterparts. Near the end of my time there, my socialization paid dividends in terms of acceptance, but it wasn't always clear when to say yes or no to those gestures. Every spring the Chilean Navy celebrates the anniversary of a naval battle during the War of the Pacific in 1898 off the coast of Iquique in which Capitán Arturo Prat, the commander of the *Esmeralda*, along with Sargento Juan de Dios Aldea, leapt aboard a Peruvian warship, the *Huascar*, and were immediately killed in the process. Prat and Aldea are national heroes, and on May 21 each year, all the Chilean Navy officers around Valparaíso muster at their units, eat a simple dinner like Prat would have eaten aboard ship during the War of the Pacific, and hear a reading of the history of the battle and the sacrifices of Prat and Aldea. At midnight, all the officers gather in full dress blues with sabers at the Plaza Sotomayor in downtown Valparaíso where the statue of Chile's naval heroes is located and ceremonially salute with their sabers. The foreign officers who attend Escuela de Guerra are invited to the ceremony but are not allowed to bring their swords or sabers.[2] To my knowledge, I was the only foreign officer allowed to wear a sword at the Plaza Sotomayor, and I was proud to do so. I was also invited by Comandante Del Real to march in a parade with the destacamento near

---

2. A saber typically has a hand guard and is curved. A sword has a straight blade and no hand guard. The US Marine Corps Mameluke sword is slightly curved, but has no handguard.

the end of my tour in Chile. I took it as a genuine gesture of trust and acceptance and was flattered, but after I thought through it, I turned him down. My reasoning was extremely simple. Parades in the Chilean military are serious business, highly photographed and publicized, and very public. When the Chileans (of any military service, including the national police) pass in review, they goose-step. Although several countries' militaries do this in parades, we North Americans immediately associate the goose-step with Hitler's Nazis. The optics of a US Marine goose-stepping in his green dress uniform alongside the Chilean Marines in their blue uniforms would have been catastrophic in the US, even though this occurred before the proliferation of social media platforms that would have enabled the images to easily go viral. There would be no explanation or context that could have made that okay, and many people would have accused me of totally going native and shaming my country. Now, I always saluted the Chilean flag along with everyone else at morning formation and when the national anthem was sung. It is not a pledge of allegiance, of course. It is a recognition of the national sovereignty in the country where you happen to be.

Because Margaret spoke virtually no Spanish when we moved to Chile, she didn't start to get up to speed on socializing until about six months into our time there. For her birthday I bought her a nice tennis racket and some lessons at the Club Naval. She was not only an All-Decade All-Conference volleyball player in college; she is a lifelong natural athlete who excels at whatever sport she picks up.[3] She started out in the "C" bracket at the Club Naval. She thrived on the lessons and matches on the clay courts at Viña, but more importantly, she took the time to have coffee with the other ladies in the club, who kindly went out of their way to befriend her and orient her to life in Chile. Her Spanish took off, as did her socialization and her enjoyment of our overseas experience. She is, in athletic terms, a gamer: someone who does okay in practice but plays several levels higher in a game when the lights shine brighter and the collars get tighter. When it came tournament time, she inexplicably trounced players she had been paired with in practice, eventually working her way well into the "A" bracket. When

---

3. I often thought that if I gave her a set of bocce balls on Christmas morning, she'd be world-class by New Year's Day.

the tennis ladies went to the country for a weekend retreat, they wrote and performed songs about one another, which seems to be a custom that is encoded in Chilean DNA. The stanza about Margaret contained something like, "La gringa alta de la tierra lejana, ¡puta madre! Siempre gana" (The tall gringa from the faraway land, son of a bitch! She always wins).

The main ingredient for Margaret's rapid learning was play, and I'm convinced that's a factor in why children also learn language so rapidly.[4] Before JD could correctly conjugate verbs, he would try to use them ungrammatically in the infinitive form while talking to other kids because he was so desperate to play. But his Spanish rapidly improved. By the time we had been there about eight months, I overheard another kid ask him where he got a toy that he was playing with. Without any hesitation, JD answered, "Mi abuela me lo dio" (My grandmother gave it to me) without any hint of North American accent. In just that short phrase, he correctly employed the vocabulary, possessive, gender, an irregular verb in the preterit, the correct use of preterit versus imperfect, and double object pronouns (the syntax of which is the total reverse of English); all things that are hard for many nonnative-speaking senior-level college Spanish majors to correctly do.

JD was helped out enormously in his language development and acculturation by attending Mackay School in Viña. Regarded as the best boys' school in town, it had cachet as the "English" school, with a Welsh headmaster, bilingual classes, and English-language signage around campus. The school day would start with the teacher saying, "Good morning, class." They would respond, "Good morning, meess (miss)," and then shift to mostly Spanish for the rest of the day. Mackay School was pronounced "mah-KAee" by Chileans. Students at Mackay School, known as "Mackayinos," wore blue blazers with the school crest sewn on, striped ties, white shirts, gray slacks, and black shoes. There were also navy-blue school coveralls and a blue school sweatsuit for sports. We had a terrible time trying to figure out which uniform JD was supposed to wear when. During the first few weeks, many were the mornings we showed up in one uniform, realized he had the wrong one, and turned around and walked home to change. JD's Spanish

---

4. There is a host of other factors, such as brain plasticity, that account for this "age-window" of optimal language learning.

and English reading and writing skills were boosted by the hard work of a skilled and dedicated teacher named Claudia, who tutored him after school several days a week during his first year. By the time we left Chile, both boys could speak just like Chilean kids their age with exactly the same accent, intonation, and slang.

Birthday parties are part of the glue that holds Chilean society together. At JD's school the birthday parties always involved inviting the whole class. There was apparently no "I don't want to invite this person." The party format was nearly universal, with slight variations in the gift opening. At some parties, you'd hand over the gift to the birthday kid at the door and she/he would rip into it right there. At others, the gifts went into a big pile, and at some point, everyone would sit down and the parents would pull gifts out one at a time. When a gift was produced from the pile, the kids would sing out, in unison, "¿De quién será?" (Who is it from?). Then they'd read the name of the giver from the little card attached to the present. Then the kids would start to chant in unison "¡Que lo abra!" (Open it!) in an ecstatic crescendo until the birthday kid would rip into it. The zenith of the birthday party occurred after the singing of Feliz Cumpleaños and the blowing out of candles. The kids would shout in unison "¡Tortazo!"[5] over and over until someone would forcefully push the birthday kid's face into the cake. I was sensitive as a kid and I'm sure a tortazo would have traumatized me for the rest of my life, but the Chilean kids take it in stride. The tortazo is so universal and anticipated that bakeries in Chile will make you a birthday cake with a sheet of wax paper under the top layer of icing to protect against any unhygienic aftereffects. Throughout the parties, the kids would drink seemingly limitless amounts of Coke, which was a little problematic for us since we tried to limit the amount of Coke for our kids. Coke may be decried as "the black water of imperialism" in large parts of Latin America, but it was almost universally drunk in Chile, from filling baby bottles to mixing with pisco for adults, to being chugged while smoking a cigarette between tennis matches by women in Margaret's league at the Club Naval.

---

5. *Torta* is "cake" and the -azo augmentative suffix denotes "a big ole" version of something. We have no equivalent word in English for the act of having one's face smashed into one's own birthday cake.

Our younger son, Jackson, attended a preschool called Greentown where the teachers were addressed as Tía (Aunt). A few months before we left, he graduated to pre-kinder at MacKay School. He was so proud to wear the school uniform and be identified as a mackayino. He developed an expansive vocabulary littered with words ending in the diminutive suffixes of *−ito* and *−ita*. There was strong emphasis at Greentown on art, and Jackson caught the bug to such a degree that he would empty the computer printer of paper to supply his projects. Both boys' schools stressed *compañerismo* (essentially the discipline of being a good classmate), and their report cards included grades in this area that counted just as heavily as individual academic performance.

My parents came to visit and loved every bit of Chile they were able to see and experience. When we drove along the rocky coast between Viña and Concón, my mother asked me if there was ever a time when we drove that road that it didn't occur to me how beautiful it was. I confessed that there was not. As we drove around the towns and past the fields and vineyards in the country, my father asked me dozens of insightful questions about the economy, trade, crops, and commerce that had never occurred to me. His point of view made me question what I was thinking about and if I was thinking anything at all when I was seeing the same things.

Before we left to go to Chile, someone who had lived overseas recommended to me that I find an English-speaking church to attend if possible. We joined Union Church, which used to be Scotch Presbyterian before becoming a Vineyard church in the '90s. The Vineyard was big on demonstrative expressions of worship, which was different than what we were used to as Baptists. A lot of folks would close their eyes and raise their hands while singing and praying, and one well-dressed lady would leave her pew weeping and crawl/drag herself to the altar on most Sundays. The pastors were English-speaking missionary pastors from the UK and the US, and the whole church seemed to be strongly bilingual, although near the end of our time there the church started to phase into nearly all Spanish to reach more Chileans. In addition to the great comfort of being able to worship and socialize in English for a few hours, we made great friends and grew to love Union Church, which was as institutionally and culturally social as everything else Chilean. The entire church went on weekend-long retreats where we shared wine and potluck meals, played soccer, and baptized new believers in the swimming pool. The men's group often met at a pub downtown.

Even businesses seemed to operate on the basis of personal relationships rather than economic efficiency. If you ever, exasperated by customer dissatisfaction, brandished your money and told a business in Chile that you plan to go spend that money with their competitor, you would probably be immediately shown the door. They don't care about losing you as a client, but they do care about losing you as a friend.

None of this sociability made great sense in terms of efficiency, but it was tremendously pragmatic because it strengthened the relationships which lubricated the gearing of how things got done. So, although our sense of how much time it takes to do something had to be adjusted to a slower setting in Chile, it had to again be recalibrated for the businesslike approach to social encounters when we returned to the States.

It's Not That Cheap

Gastón Arriagada was the commandant of the Chilean Marine Corps when I was there. He was a tall, charismatic guy famous for assigning tough training missions to his subordinate commanders. Legend had it that he'd tell a company commander to go patrol or attack a unit at a certain point and give him precious little time to get there, invariably through a swamp or thicket in the dark of night. The young lieutenants' hearts would sink as Arriagada, with a casual wave of his broad hand over a 1:50,000 scale map, would describe the assigned missions. Sensing their dread, Arriagada tended to tell them that if they couldn't do the mission, he'd send a platoon of bakers[1] to do it. In recognition and perhaps recompense for having authorized and funded the unplanned hosting of the shipwrecked US Marines back in September of 2000, Arriagada was invited to tour part of the East Coast Marine Corps. He was authorized to bring his Aide de Camp and his G3 (operations officer). I was to go as the escort officer. We flew on a commercial flight to Miami, where we were met by the US Southern Command[2] Foreign Liaison Officer, Comandante Hartung. We then took military flights to Parris Island, South Carolina, and Camp Lejeune, North Carolina.

---

1. There were bakers in the destacamento, and when we went to the field they would produce about four thousand pieces of pan amasado daily in a kitchen under canvas.

2. Southern Command (SOUTHCOM) is one of the regionally focused joint commands that coordinates US military-to-military interaction with countries of Latin America and the Caribbean. A joint command is one staffed by people from all the military services.

Figure 3: Welcoming Contraalmirante Gastón Arriagada to Destacamento Miller. From left to right: Capitán de Navío Cristián Del Real, Arriagada, Capitán de Fragata Roberto Opazo, Capitán de Fragata Cristián Wunderlich, Major Mark McGraw, and Capitán de Corbeta Eduardo Aranda.

Flavio Montagna, the admiral's aide de camp, was a sharp guy and a gifted joke teller. He had a phenomenal memory and could recite, to the quarter hour, the entire schedule of a three-day visit of some dignitary, down to the uniform to be worn at each function. I suspect he also took a short article I wrote in pretty rudimentary Spanish for the Chilean Marine newsletter and tuned it up into a sonorous wonder worthy of the language of Cervantes, but I could never get him to admit it.

Comandante Jorge Ureta, a burly guy with a broom moustache, had been the exchange officer to the US Marines years before, and being a commando, did some training with the recon units on the West Coast, so we knew a lot of the same people in the US Marine Corps. Arriagada trusted him and valued his opinion, and whenever we saw a demonstration or received a briefing on something, Ureta would tell him what he thought, what it might mean for the Chilean Marine Corps, and how transportable or valuable it might or might not be if adapted for use by the Chilean Marines. The Chilean Marines started out as coastal artillery with a fundamentally defensive mission, but had morphed into an amphibious force sometime in the 1960s. They shamelessly copied the US Marines wherever resources allowed.

At Parris Island, we saw varied aspects of recruit training, nothing new to Arriagada since he had commanded Chilean Marine recruit training in Talcahuano. What did catch his eye was the recently revamped Marine Corps Water Survival Test, which focused on preparing Marines to survive and move themselves through the water while wearing all their gear. Arriagada used the past participle "guevada" as a noun to characterize what the Chilean Marines had been doing for water survival testing up to that point. Preparations were immediately made to copy and paste a version of the same test into the Chilean Marine annual training.

Our host for the Camp Lejeune part of the visit was Lieutenant General Martin R. Berndt. Marty Berndt, who died in 2011, was a prince of a guy with big Popeye forearms who gained fame in 1995 as a colonel commanding the Marine Expeditionary Unit that rescued Scott O'Grady, a US Air Force pilot who had ejected from his F-16C over a hostile part of Bosnia. After a short flight on a military aircraft from Parris Island to New River Airfield near Camp Lejeune, we taxied up the runway and saw General Berndt standing out on the tarmac saluting. The ranks between the two flag-rank officers were kind of a mismatch: Berndt was a three-star. Arriagada a one-star, but he was the commandant of his nation's Marine Corps, which connoted special status for US Marines. Berndt treated Arriagada as an honored guest, which deeply impressed Arriagada. Even though they had to communicate through interpreters, Berndt and Arriagada hit it off.

The afternoon we got to Camp Lejeune, we checked in to the newly remodeled Bachelor Officer Quarters. Arriagada was billeted in a separate house nearby for generals. He was thirsty from the long trip, drank water out of the tap, and became immediately sick, the exact geographical opposite of what you might think would happen to a gringo traveling in Latin America. I'm no environmental health expert, but it seems to me that all drinking water everywhere has some amount of creepy crawlies in it. It's just that

I've grown used to mine and you've gotten accustomed to yours. We took him to the Camp Lejeune hospital, where he was treated for colitis. It was my first time to interpret for someone in a medical emergency. Arriagada rode sidesaddle for a couple of days after that, but he eventually was none the worse for wear.

Part of our Camp Lejeune visit included a stop at a giant maintenance hangar at the Force Service Support Group. As we were walking around this workshop where about sixty US Marines were turning wrenches, Flavio Montagna pointed out a US Marine corporal and said, "Ese tipo tiene cara chilena" (That guy has a Chilean face), which of course meant to say that he had an indigenous face. When they went up to him and asked where he was from, it turned out he had indeed been born in Temuco, Chile.

Now, when a Chilean takes a trip to the US, she or he will be given by friends and family members a list as long as your arm. These are the encargos: items that can be bought in the US that are prohibitively expensive or inexistent in Chile. The list will be sufficiently voluminous to require the traveler to purchase two additional pieces of luggage to carry back all the loot. At the time, Chile put an eighteen percent value-added tax on imported products (they may still). Some items like well-made MP3 players (cutting-edge technology at the time) couldn't even be bought in Chile. The legends about how cheap things were in the US grew as they passed from person to person. Chileans are great exaggerators and they'd pass right over the word *barato* (cheap) and call the things they could get in the US *botado* (thrown out, essentially given away to whomever would haul the item off) or *regalado* (given away). The value-added tax on imported items in Chile was one of those things that created a curious Chilean mentality that assumed everything was cheaper, better, easier, more developed, and more prosperous in the US. I will readily concede that my countrymen and I have plenty of flaws in our own collective national mentality (if such a thing exists), but I found this Chilean article of faith that there was another country in the same hemisphere where everything was better to be especially crippling and pessimism-fostering.

The Chilean linguistic anglophilia still strongly manifests itself in Chilean marketing. In 2018 our friends the Fierros tried to walk through an entire shopping mall in Santiago to see if they could find a storefront that didn't have any signage, brands, labels or communications in English. They couldn't find a single one. I bought handmade leather shoes at a store where the motto, "Made in Chile, not in China" was proudly displayed in the exact English I have written here, blissfully unaware of the irony of extolling Chilean workmanship in Chile in English. Curiously, the proliferation of English in Chilean advertising is not for the purpose of reaching tourists, but for appealing to Chileans themselves, who seem to uncritically or unconsciously accept that the product or company with the English-language label is inherently superior.

The Chilean officers were able to purchase a significant number of the encargos at the Camp Lejeune PX, but for the stuff their family members wanted, we needed to spend most of a Sunday afternoon at Sawgrass Mills, the giant outlet mall in Broward County on the edge of the Everglades. I passionately hate malls, so I walked around and kept myself occupied while the Chileans made forays into the mall like pirates raiding small coastal villages. At the appointed time to meet back at the car to go to the hotel, I found Arriagada and Montagna cramming armloads of merchandise in the car and, timeline be damned, they were going to make one more run into the bowels of the mall. As they turned to hustle back into the building, I overheard the admiral say to Flavio, "You know, it's really not that cheap."

No. It's not.

A New Boss and a Trip to Colombia

By New Year's 2001, we were completing our first six months in Chile. As is the custom in Latin American militaries, the new calendar year brings new assignments, and the most meaningful ones for me were the departure of my friend, sponsor, and carreta, Francisco Fierro, and the arrival of a new comandante, Cristián Del Real Pérez. Del Real had a reputation as a workaholic and demanding boss. He was in pretty good shape, a compact guy, with a high forehead and aquiline nose that reminded me of portraits I had seen of Simón Bolívar, South America's George Washington. He was intensely nationalistic for reasons I figured out later.

As soon as Del Real took over, I was told to move out of the head-quarters building where I shared an office with the new operations officer, Cristián Wunderlich (the younger brother of my former comandante). Del Real had Wunderlich give me the news. It was a gut punch. Although my job responsibilities didn't change on paper, I was moved out of the headquarters to an empty office next to the Batallón de Fusileros—the Rifle Battalion, where for a while I had nothing to do, no contact with the destacamento headquarters, and no role in the planning of training and operations. I found out later that at the SOUTHCOM Headquarters in Miami, Del Real's friend Rodrigo Sánchez (along with all the other international officers) was similarly isolated from the main headquarters, where he had succeeded Jorge Hartung as the foreign liaison officer for the Chilean military. Sánchez, the most famous loudmouth and hothead in the Chilean Marines at that time, was not one to suffer quietly or gracefully. When I heard about Sánchez's complaints about being kept out of the SOUTHCOM Headquarters, it all made perfect sense. It was quid pro quo to exile me from the destacamento command post, and it also let me know they didn't think I had enough to contribute to warrant being in the office spaces where all the plans were being made. Whether they be gestures of generosity or exclusion by North Americans, Latin Americans are almost guaranteed to reciprocate.

Part of the daily routine at the unit was lunch, which we would have together at 1:30 p.m. in the officers' mess. The food was generally pretty simple, but the plates were served by majordomos and the whole process involved forty-five minutes to an hour, plenty of time to converse. Sitting down for a long lunch seems to be a basic human right in Chile, and the ritual is more about group cohesion than eating a meal quickly or efficiently. You take your time and savor abundant conversation along with the food. In Santiago you'll even see deliverymen and truck drivers park on grassy medians in the middle of traffic and dine at folding tables with reusable plates, glasses, and silverware. One reason lunch is so important is that breakfast is not. You may have a little hard roll with your café con leche in the morning, and that's about it. And snacking on the job seems to be a cardinal sin. In addition to being bored, I would get hungry sitting in my new empty office alone all morning with nothing to do, so I would bring a piece of pan amasado or an apple to tide me over until lunchtime. One morning I was eating my piece of bread while reading a manual, and a Chilean Marine knocked on the door. I told him to come in and his response to seeing me snacking couldn't have been any different than if he had walked in on me naked.

At lunch the senior officers at the destacamento would hold court, expounding on subjects both personal and professional and asking questions around the table. My first few months there, I usually kept my mouth shut for fear of saying something foolish or grossly ungrammatical. And even though my comprehension level for one-on-one Spanish was pretty good, being the only foreigner at a table with six or seven Chileans was a whole different ballgame. Having known one another professionally and personally for years, they could talk to one another almost in shorthand, referring to events and institutions and other people well-known to them by nicknames, acronyms, and abbreviations. And to be "competitive" conversationally, to contribute to the discussion and be heard, people had to speak rapidly. All those factors conspired to leave me in a cold outer orbit of incomprehension, but I would be politely pulled into the discussion with an occasional question. When Walter Wunderlich was the comandante, he would make efforts to include me in the conversation and Francisco Fierro was usually right next to me to explain some points or provide conversational footnotes in Spanish, but with a speed and vocabulary that I could take on board.

That helpfulness temporarily stopped when Del Real took over and Francisco transferred to Talcahuano. When Del Real and I wound up at the same lunch table, which was the most common arrangement since we were among the most senior four or five people in the unit, he seemed to intentionally exclude me from the conversation, taking care to visually engage everyone at the table but me when he talked. The tables were round and seated about eight people, so you had to work at it to ignore someone. I don't know if he was convinced I didn't understand anything or if he wanted to make the point to the other officers that I was to be treated as no big deal. I guess it was the first time in my life I felt purposefully excluded, treated as if I probably understood nothing and had nothing to contribute, as if I were a potted plant. I felt unmoored and isolated and I started to dread my remaining time at the destacamento, since Del Real would be the comandante for the rest of my time in Chile. The low point was one week when we were in the field training and a friend of his, another Navy officer, dropped by. Del Real courteously introduced me to the visitor with some reference that I might be a spy from the empire to the north.

Our relationship, and my situation in the destacamento, took a turn when Del Real and I went to Colombia together for a planning conference. In 2001 the US-led Navy exercise in Latin America known as UNITAS changed formats from US-led and organized, to regionally led, starting with Colombia. The Colombian Navy and Marines would plan the exercise, invite nearby countries to participate, and take the lead on executing the exercise through a fictional scenario. The Chilean Navy was invited to participate, so I wound up accompanying a group of Chilean officers to Bogotá for a planning conference. There were five or six Chileans, including Comandante Del Real, and me, the lone gringo. We were billeted at a Colombian military complex and driven around in a van by a Colombian civilian driver.

One thing I found out about Chileans, at least Chilean Navy guys, on this trip was that they, like Mormon missionaries, go everywhere together. There was no "Hey, you guys go on and have a good time. I'll get a cab and go somewhere different," or "I don't feel like going out, so I'll just hang here at the hotel." For me, being about as individualistic as any other North American, spending every waking moment of my free time with a group took some getting used to. For our group the most senior guy would decide where we'd go for meals and activities and everyone else would just fall right into line and get on the van at the appointed time. A guy about my age, Jorge Palacios, desperately wanted to eat at a hamburger–hot dog place called Corral, and he repeatedly expressed his preference to whomever the senior guy was. I don't know how much it was just to keep Palacios in his place as the junior guy, but we didn't eat at Corral until the last meal.

We arrived at Bogotá on the weekend and the first place Del Real wanted to go was to mass. He knew I wasn't Catholic and told me I didn't have to go to mass if I didn't want to, but I wanted to attend. We went to Saturday evening mass in a beautiful cathedral in the center of Bogotá. In the van afterward I told him that except for some of the ceremonial aspects of mass, it was a lot like the church services I go to, and that the homily was just about the same as a sermon I would hear in my church in the States, just in Spanish. He seemed a little surprised by that.

I learned that my inability to fully comprehend Chilean Spanish was not totally my fault. In Bogotá they speak some of the most pure, standard, comprehensible Spanish in the world and our Colombian driver had trouble understanding the Chileans, too, a fact that gave me enormous satisfaction and a little shot of self-esteem.

I also found out it was considered unsafe to travel alone in Bogotá wearing a US military uniform. Several of the Chileans wanted to change their return flights, so I offered to go to the US embassy travel office to try to exchange the tickets. I hailed a cab from the complex where we were living and working and told them to take me to the US embassy a few miles away. Outside the embassy walls there was a long line of people waiting to enter, so I saw nothing else to do but to take my place in line with my military ID and plane tickets in hand. A few minutes later an armored embassy vehicle passed by; the driver, a security officer, did a double take and jammed on the brakes, and then backed up to come alongside me. "What are you doing out here?" he yelled before handing me a Kevlar vest, telling me to put it on and yelling at me to get in the vehicle. He then drove me inside the walls through a different gate. The guy told me that the FARC and ELN[1] were active in the capital and would have loved to have a chance to kill or kidnap a US military guy in broad daylight.

I later pieced together some things about Del Real that might explain his initial aloofness and unfriendliness. The US Marine officer who had been in my job several years before was an apparent dud, famous for learning very little Spanish during his two years in Chile. Del Real had no use for the guy and probably anticipated that I would be about the same, since I wasn't a native speaker of Spanish, either. Another factor was that, unlike 99.99 percent of the officers who were active in the Navy at the time I was in Chile, Del Real didn't attend the Chilean Naval Academy. When the armed forces seized power on September 11, 1973, Del Real was in the reserves and was attending a regular university. He immediately reported for and was placed on active duty, but in a tense environment where a perceived lack of total loyalty to the Pinochet regime could have fatal consequences, he needed to be hyper-nationalistic, which even twenty years later didn't square with cozying up to a foreign guy, especially a North American Marine.

A lot of the older officers harbored some antipathy toward the US, which is understandable when you know the history. Our CIA supported the coup in 1973 and in the early '70s large segments of our national security apparatus supported the Pinochet regime because they were glad to have Salvador Allende, a socialist president, taken off the map in Latin America. But the emphasis on human rights during the Jimmy Carter administration turned off that support, and the Democratic majority in Congress during the Reagan years starved the Chilean military of supplies, arms, and repair parts to maintain the gear that we had sold them, leaving them high and dry during a tense border standoff with Argentina. In 1978, Del Real spent nearly a year in the freezing cold in Patagonia with gear that didn't work

---

1. Fuerzas Armadas Revolucionarias de Colombia (Revolutionary Armed Forces of Colombia) and Ejército de Liberación Nacional (National Liberation Army)

because the US refused to send repair parts. I knew none of this history when I was starting to get to know him.

Another factor that helped me on the trip to Colombia was that Del Real wasn't always the senior guy when we went somewhere. The Chilean naval attaché to Colombia, a guy whose name escapes me, but had incredibly long hair even for a Navy guy, outranked him. That meant that he, and not Del Real, controlled the conversation when we went to dinner and rode around in the van. The attaché showed enough interest in me and let me talk enough for Del Real to see that I was a decent guy and could speak Spanish well enough to hold my own socially. I didn't know it at the time, but I was developing my own approach for how to represent myself, my Marine Corps, and my country when I was in Chile. I decided not to try to be an apologist for everything people would dredge up to hold against the US. I usually was not linguistically capable of an intense debate in Spanish, anyway. It seemed that the best I could do was spend as much time with the Chileans as possible, be myself, listen more than talk, and share opinions and experiences with them without being preachy. I couldn't make them like the US, but most of the time, if they took the time to get to know me or my family, they would like us on a personal level to some degree. And since in many cases we were the only North Americans they knew, they based a lot of how they felt about the US on how they felt about us.

I knew for sure that the trip had changed the relationship between Del Real and me because the Monday morning after we got back from the trip to Colombia, I found out he told the staff he wanted to make me the commander of the Rifle Battalion, basically the ground combat element of the destacamento. The staff convinced him that he couldn't do it. Someone produced a copy of the memorandum of agreement between the US Marine Corps and the Chilean Marine Corps signed back in 1990 when the exchange program started. The agreement prohibited the foreign officer from commanding troops in the host nation's Marine Corps, a stipulation that makes abundant good sense when one considers all that is involved in military command (in Chile it even included interviewing potential spouses of junior officers). So I stayed in my jobs of assistant operations officer, training officer, and fire support coordinator, and Del Real started to give me much more responsibility around the unit, even though I never moved my office back into the main headquarters.

Del Real and I eventually came to be as close and friendly as any senior/subordinate military officers can be. We traded books and talked about leadership and tactics. When we were embarked on ship and sailed past something interesting, he'd call for me so he could point it out and give me background on it. Near the end of my time in Chile, when we were out training in the field, another friend of Del Real's came by to visit. Del Real introduced me as "Comandante McGraw, tan chileno como los porotos" (Commander McGraw, as Chilean as beans), a common Chilean phrase used to indicate that something is totally national and homegrown.

Desafío

Every year near the end of the vacation period of January to February, the Chilean Marine commandos sponsored an adventure race similar to Eco-Challenge[1] or Raid Gauloises.[2] The commandos' version in 2001 was called *Desafío* (Challenge). The event encompassed four or five days of traversing about three hundred kilometers of rough country from checkpoint to checkpoint on foot, on bicycle, on horseback, by rubber raft in the open ocean, swimming, ascending a cliff by jumar ascender, and descending a cliff by rappelling. Five-person teams were to be mixed, and all of them had four men and one woman, even though a team could have had any combination of men and women. Team composition was crucial because if a single member had to drop out or couldn't complete an event, it wasn't a time penalty, it was total disqualification. I don't remember if I asked to be part of the team, or if I was offered an opportunity to compete for a spot on the team, but I don't think I was actively recruited. As usual, since I'm not Chilean, questions were initially raised as to whether I could participate, but they were put to rest and I started training with the team. Long gone were the days when I had 7 percent body fat and could run three miles in under eighteen minutes, but I was still in pretty good shape in 2001 and I wanted to do an event like this. I thought of it as a long patrol, and I had done plenty of those.

---

1. Eco-Challenge, created in 1992 by Mark Burnett of the reality TV series *Survivor* fame, was run until 2002. As of the publication of this book, the Eco-Challenge race has been revived and is ongoing.
2. The Raid Gauloises, generally accepted as the original adventure race, was named for its first sponsor, a French cigarette company. The raid eventually became the Adventure Race World Series.

A couple of the other guys on the team, Mauricio Troncoso and Felipe Alvear, had experience in the event from the year before, but Victor Vivanco and I were rookies. Mauricio was a *cabo* (corporal), probably in his mid-to-late twenties, and he reminded me of the young US Marines I knew from the US Marine reconnaissance battalions. He was outspoken, opinionated, and sure of himself, for good reason. He was talented, tough, and capable. Felipe was a *sargento*, older, perhaps as old as I was (37 at the time). He liked to repeat the only phrase he knew in English, "Oh my God" (but he pronounced it "Gott" like it was German). Victor was a *cabo segundo*, in his midtwenties. He was skinny and funny. We constantly wore camelback hydration systems in training: backpacks with a sleeve where you kept as much as a hundred ounces of water in a flexible bladder. As unappetizing as it may sound to drink water out of something called a bladder, the camelback was a lifesaver, since you can carry such a large quantity of water close to your body and have ready access to it through a hose that runs from the bladder over your shoulder. At times Victor would sing the chorus of an incredibly cheesy pop song from the '70s, "Mi amigo Charlie Brown," which he adapted to express his love and fascination for his camelback (which Chileans pronounced "CAHmelvack"), which I found entertaining no matter how tired I was. Someone recruited a female sailor, Carolina Toloza, who worked at the hospital in Viña, to round out our team. I think she had trained with a team, but I don't remember if she had actually done Desafío before. She was young and in good health, but was not an athlete, and when we started training she soon started to develop the classic overuse injuries associated with someone who does too much too soon.

The destacamento was in a holding pattern since it was vacation time. Comandante Del Real was on vacation and the segundo comandante, a funny guy whom I liked a lot when we were off duty, was in charge. I don't know if it was the logistical support we occasionally requested from the unit or the fact that an officer and some enlisted Marines were running around in shorts on bicycles during the training day, but the segundo comandante didn't like the Desafío training at all. Requests for support or funding for our team were met with rolled eyes and reminders from him that our raison d'être was to win in combat, not to ride around on bicycles. Consistent with

Figure 4: Before the start of Desafío, with Margaret and most of our team and support guys. Our last team member, Carolina Toloza, was waiting in a boat just beyond the surf. From left to right: Sargento Nicolás Araya, Cabo Victor Vivanco, Cabo Mauricio Troncoso, Major Mark McGraw, Margaret McGraw, Sargento Felipe Alvear, and Sargento Eduardo Burgueño.

what one experiences when dealing with any bureaucracy, we generally got about two-thirds of what we asked for, and always after extensive explanations and justification.

We spent February training for Desafío. Our training most days, a glorious alternative to sitting around the office all day trying to look busy, consisted of going out on our mountain bikes and exploring the gravel roads around Viña and Concón, places well-known to the guys, but mostly new to me. Since the chow hall was not open for lunch when we would leave for training, we'd get sack lunches delivered by a sergeant, Nicolás Araya, who was always called by the fabulous name of his hometown, Punitaqui. The preponderance of the previous year's course had been covered by bike, so we made cycling the focus of our preparation. None of our bikes were anything special, although mine was probably a little better than theirs. One day during training we had to cross a barbed-wire fence and when I lifted my bike over to Felipe, he hoisted it and grinned knowingly to the other team members as if he had caught me cheating. "¡Es una pluma!" (It's a feather) he exclaimed. The critical shortfall of our bikes was the poor quality of the tires and tubes most of us had. The enlisted guys didn't have much money to spend on tires and tubes, so those were some of the items we asked the destacamento to fund. As a result, we had the cheapest tubes possible and we tried to patch them (often a losing proposition) whenever possible. Mountain bike tire technology has come a long way since 2001. No serious mountain bike rider even runs tubes in his or her tires anymore, opting for tubeless tire systems that use sealant, much like car tires. The environment of mountain biking, especially in Chile with the rocky trails and thorn bushes, is prone to puncture tubes.

As part of our preparation, we practiced paddling a rubber boat and made sure we swam well enough to complete those parts of the competition. Carolina was a weak swimmer and Mauricio and I were the strongest, so we also practiced towing her by attaching sections of parachute cord to our UDT vests.[3] We practiced rappelling and climbing with the jumar, an aluminum device a little bigger than a fist that clamps down on a climbing rope and then releases to allow you to slide the device up. You use these in a pair, one for each hand and one higher than the other. The higher jumar will be attached to a sling around your legs that you essentially sit in. The lower jumar has a sling attached to the bottom of it with a loop for one of your feet. The technique of ascending is a little awkward because you're moving your left foot and left arm upward at the same time. You allow the jumar in the left hand to clamp down on the rope as you stand on the loop with the foot on the same side. Then you let the jumar in the other hand slide up with the slack you create by standing. Clamp, stand, unclamp, bend, slide up, clamp, stand.

The only parts of the training that were not fun for me were the few occasions when we went running. Now, there was not an event in the Desafío that had to do specifically with running, and the prospect of running the three hundred kilometers with backpacks was preposterous, but you always

---

3. UDT (Underwater Demolition Team) vests were inflatable with either a CO_2 cartridge or oral inflation tube. You wore them deflated when in a boat or swimming.

had the option to run a section if everyone could do it. The run training was valuable, though, in that it had to do with propelling your own body weight over a designated distance, and that had everything to do with Desafío. Except for Carolina, I was the slowest runner of the bunch even though I had about a dozen marathons under my belt at that time and was generally good for twenty minutes for the three-mile run. I got better with training, but I was still the slowest.

The competition started, in reality, the day before we crossed the start line. We checked in and were given the rules and, most importantly, the maps with the checkpoints in the order that we had to hit them. Mauricio and Felipe immediately commented that the course seemed to be harder than the year before, and they started planning the route while we staged our equipment and had it inspected by the race officials. As was the case with many training days, we spent a lot of time just sitting around waiting for what was next, and we had a lot of time to talk. In some ways I found myself starting over at almost zero in understanding what was said around me. Just like in the US military (probably all militaries to one degree or another), the officer and enlisted ranks were generally comprised of people from different socioeconomic backgrounds, so the language was different due to what linguists call social register. The vocabulary used by my teammates was different and the vocabulary of the competition was new to me. We were given a set of instructions and a punch card similar to what would be used in orienteering to get official credit for hitting our checkpoints. We put them in a heavy plastic bag and attached a string to it so that one of us could carry it around the neck at all times. A near panic ensued mid-race when one of them asked me if I had the "bases." I didn't know what they were asking about so I just said no. I didn't know what was being asked, but I was pretty sure I didn't have what they were asking. What they were calling the "bases" was the critically important waterproofed card with the checkpoints on it. I would have called it anything else. The more tired I got, the harder it was to speak and understand. And Desafío, as the name implied, was all about being tired.

We started the competition swimming through the cold surf at the beach at Viña out to waiting rubber Zodiac boats that were rafted up a couple of hundred meters beyond the surf zone. We paddled north to Concón. Since we could see the other teams and people could see us from the shore, we went stupidly hard. Since the commandos, the organizers of the competition, had a team that was nearly unbeatable year in and year out, I don't think we believed we had any chance to win, but Mauricio, Felipe, and Victor, being commandos and wanting to give good accounts of themselves, wanted to finish in the top three teams. I'm not sure what Carolina's competition goals were, but I just wanted to complete the event. We paddled like mad for a few miles up the coast to Concón, where our boat was summarily flipped in the heavy surf as we approached the beach. Once on dry land we quickly got our socks and shoes on and started running up the beach with our packs on. For a multiday three-hundred-kilometer race, the level of speed and effort we were putting in was foolish, but I was loath to dampen anyone's enthusiasm. Eventually we turned from the coast inland over dunes of deep sand. My shoes immediately filled up with so much sand that I felt like I was wearing Frankenstein shoes. I asked that we stop a couple of times to dump them out.

After hiking all day and evening we got to the rope climb and rappel in the middle of the night. We managed to get them done with no major problems, even though we had not practiced those skills in the dark. I remember Carolina getting angry at the jumars setup while she was trying to climb, exasperatedly yelling "¡Esta cuestión!" (This thing!). It was the closest she ever came to using bad language that I heard.

We ate wild grapes near a place called El Coipo and slept a little bit before passing through Portezuelo Ocoa and climbing up to a hilltop known as La Campana in the center of a national park by the same name. Campana's summit is at 6,300 feet above sea level, and on a clear day the same breakers that flipped our rubber boat at Concón are visible from the summit. Somewhere near Portezuelo on a long, steep climb we passed or were passed by another team. They were towing their female team member by a piece of parachute cord tied to one wrist. If the context of the competition were stripped away, an observer would think that she was being abducted, but she looked as content as if she were on her way to happy hour on a cruise.

Sometime the next day we got to where our bikes were staged. I was thrilled at the prospect of traveling fast while sitting my butt on a seat, albeit a small one. We ripped out of that checkpoint single file up a gravel road on our bikes, where the thrill of finally being bicycle-mobile died a quick death on a hill too steep for any of us to ride. We dutifully hiked our bikes in the cruel sun until the trail topped out and we could start riding again. Riding hard and fast on rocky terrain soon produced a series of flat tires. If you're running tubes in your tires, hitting a rock hard enough will produce a flat where the soft rubber tube is pinched between the sharp obstacle and the unyielding tire rim. At a point early in a three-hundred-kilometer race where we should have been covering ground at fifteen to eighteen miles per hour, we were stock still for what felt like eons trying to repair flats. Some of the flats were so bad that the sidewalls of the tires themselves were compromised. Within a quarter mile of fixing one of Felipe's flats I remember wondering about the provenance of an odd repetitive noise before Felipe's tube, which had pushed through a cut in the sidewall like a giant pimple, exploded like a gunshot. We arranged a sidewall support[4] to get him rolling for a while before someone else would have a flat. Everyone wanted to help, so we would converge around the victim to hold, stow, or prepare items used in the repair. Tragedy struck when someone stepped on the tube of glue required to put the patches on the tubes. The wasted glue sat in a sad little pile in the dirty gravel and our hearts sank as teams zoomed past us on working bikes. We eventually borrowed a tube from someone and were able to keep rolling when we hit a nice road.

Our poor diet soon started to hamper us. One of the staples of our food supply was, believe it or not, horse jerky, which tasted more gamey and stringy than beef. It turns out that the word "jerky" comes from the South American Quechua word "charqui," so the act of eating horse jerky in Chile was not too far from its geographical and linguistic origin. However culturally interesting horse jerky may be, there aren't many calories in it, and it contains no carbohydrates whatsoever. The other pillar of our diet

---

4. This technique, known as using a "boot," can be accomplished using a patch, a piece of hard rubber, or even a dollar bill to keep the tube from poking through the slit in the sidewall of the tire.

was mantecool, essentially a giant candy bar that tasted like peanut butter and cocoa. Initially, mantecool tasted terrific and seemed to be promising as endurance food, but the high sugar content and the corresponding spikes and drops in insulin level started to do a number on us by the end of the second day. When we rolled into the checkpoint where we turned in our bikes to head out again on foot, Victor was "bonking" and could barely turn the pedals over. I'm a big believer in the concept of the body craving the exact things that it needs, and early in the competition I couldn't stand the taste of mantecool. What we were all wanting to eat was real food, but the closest we would ever get was some MREs[5] on the third day.

Before the competition, I was thinking that since the race was so long, it would be slow-paced. Certainly, we were moving slower than if we had been running just a 10K, but the pace was always, at least for me, well within the zone of discomfort. The lack of sleep and constant exertion were devastating for all of us. At one point in the wee hours of the morning, Carolina crashed on her bike and seemed to have a badly injured shoulder. Any toughness that years of Marine Corps training should have instilled in me, any Army Ranger School ethic of "fight on to the Ranger objective and complete the mission though I be the lone survivor,"[6] and any chivalry or impulse of basic human compassion that would have moved me to express true care for Carolina's well-being went out the window. Exhaustion had made me a selfish coward. My immediate thought was something along the lines of, "Good, now we can stop." The short-term relief of an honorable exit from the competition looked more attractive to me in that moment than finishing the competition. But she pulled herself together and we kept going. We were required by race rules to have headlights on our bikes at night, but mine was just a small blinker, designed to ensure that I was seen from the front, not bright enough so that I could see the road in front of me. So even though we got our tubes replaced and were riding on less rocky roads, our lack of night practice and my poor preparation resulted in slower times on the bike than we should have had.

---

5. US military combat rations known as Meal, Ready to Eat.
6. The last part of the Ranger Creed that Ranger students memorize and cite in training.

The bike sections, viewed through the lens of overall time instead of distance, were relatively short. The vast majority of the time we were walking, staggering along under the sun or blinking bleary-eyed in the vast darkness, stumbling on unseen rocks and broken ground. As I was to learn years later in long-distance cycling races and a multiday kayak excursion up the Wilderness Waterway in the Everglades, events this long require you to readjust your perception of time. The routine of the civilized world, the twenty-minute sermon, and the fifty-minute class period that condition you to think in chunks of minutes must be smoothed out into a broader consciousness of time: periods of daylight and darkness. We learned to be thankful for the sections of walking where we at least had a path or road, paved or otherwise. Using a global positioning system (GPS) was strictly prohibited in the competition, and we constantly referred to maps to approximate our position at any given time. When we came to a known point like a prominent road junction or hill summit, navigation was a sure thing, but we were usually moving too fast to be perfectly exact, and navigation was often a technique of "Let's just keep going in this general direction until we cross the next main road." The feeling of endless walking was probably made worse by the fact that I wasn't very familiar with the geography. Felipe and Mauricio were like the parents in the front of the car with the road map, while I was the kid in the back wondering if we were there yet. When I was plumbing the depths of exhaustion, my ability to speak and understand Spanish in the context of the competition was more and more diminished. The sounds of my teammates' voices came to me as if I were in the bottom of a deep, dark well, my brain too tired to do the hard work of connecting signifier and signified and translating the symbols of words into meaning. When I would speak, it would sound to me as if someone else were talking, and I would occasionally suspect that what I was saying made no sense. The dialogue between team members was quick, often mumbled, often a kind of shorthand between guys who had worked together for a long time. To explain something to me required speaking slower, explaining in a different way, or perhaps explaining more than once. So I again found myself inhabiting a kind of outer darkness of little communication.

One of the few pleasant and productive stretches that we covered came near Olmué after we summited La Campana for the second time. We were assigned two horses for a long stretch of good trails and roads, so we took turns riding and walking. Even when we were walking, we could put our backpacks over the horse's haunches like saddlebags, and to hike unburdened was a great luxury.

When we were on foot without the horses, many of the routes we chose took us bushwacking through rough terrain, trading the excruciation of slow movement for the promise of a shorter route. At one point we were simultaneously crossing a barbed-wire fence and climbing up a hill. One of Felipe's steps loosened a large rock that tumbled down and crushed the big toe of my right foot as I stepped through the wire. The team just looked at me in silence as I kneeled, groaned, and clutched my foot for a couple of minutes. There was nothing they could do. Besides, we were all hurting too much by then to be overly impressed by any individual's pain. We ran out of water a few times, and to this day, the sound of sucking a camelback dry takes me back to that ominous feeling of being out of water during the hottest hours of Desafío.

By the end of day three we were exhausted, filthy, hungry, scratched, and bleeding from pushing through thorn bushes and walking on blistered feet. I started to suffer from edema. My hands and lower legs were starting to swell so much that I had to loosen my watch band a couple of notches. At one of the checkpoints, an officer from another unit whom I knew from riding the van into work together told me I looked disastrously depleted. We had the good fortune to pick up some MREs on the third day at a time when we badly needed calorie-dense food. In the darkness we huddled in the tree line beside the road to wolf down our vacuum-packed food. I could hear Victor suddenly spitting frantically. I shined a flashlight on him and asked him what was wrong. He had opened a package of peanuts and, mistaking the small white package of desiccant for salt since it was too dark to see the prominent "Do Not Eat" warning printed on the side, opened it too and mixed it with the peanuts. We couldn't even catch a break sitting down to eat.

The next day we walked for miles along the Lago Peñuelas south of Quilpué. I was so tired that my mind veered drunkenly between consciousness and slumber, my vision occasionally populated by inexistent images and mirages. This was the type of bone-deep exhaustion I had experienced at Army Ranger School when I went to sleep standing up and fell into a warming fire. The body can keep functioning when extremely sleep-deprived, but the mind eventually reaches a point where it tells the body, "You can stay up if you want to; I'm going to bed." In spite of some soreness, our supposed weak link, Carolina, was doing great. By this point, the soles of her feet were covered in duct tape. She seemed to walk faster as the days wore on and I never heard her complain.

We knew that soon after we crossed Highway 68, the main road that connects Santiago to Valparaíso and Viña del Mar, we'd be doing a 2,500-meter swim across a narrow manmade lake called Embalse de la Luz. I felt good when we got to the edge of the lake at about 2 a.m. to start the swim. I had been largely useless during much of the competition, lumbering along in a haze of practical somnambulism and incomprehension, but this was where I would make good, where I would swim well enough to help tow Carolina across the lake and get onto the next stage. On a small, dimly lighted pier that marked the swim start, we put our packs into drybags and rigged them to be towed behind us. Mauricio and I rigged parachute cord to tow Carolina from the D-rings of our UDT vests, and we jumped into the water. I was shocked at how cold it was, but I figured I'd warm up soon enough and started swimming strongly. I was immediately disoriented, though, because my goggles, designed to be used in the bright sunshine, were heavily tinted. I was essentially blind. My vertigo worsened just a couple hundred yards into the swim. I switched from freestyle to breaststroke, trying to focus on the light of a boathouse at our destination, the other end of the lake. The two lines to my drybag and to Carolina started giving me the sensation of being constantly tangled in something. Then I started to have a drowning sensation as fluid seemed to come out of my lungs and into my mouth. I told Mauricio I was having trouble and he told me to let him tow me. Here we were only about halfway through the swim and I'd gone from towing someone to being towed. I pulled my goggles down around my neck, rolled over on my back, and tried to relax in hopes that I'd recover and be able to start swimming again. But the fluid being produced in my lungs (not swallowed lake water) was making it hard to breathe, contributing to the sensation of drowning. Eventually, in a near total panic of vertigo, claustrophobia, and drowning, I asked to get into the safety boat. The team, although disqualified, kept swimming without me. Only the sounds of my rattling breathing, the idling of the outboard motor of the safety boat, and the swim strokes of my teammates could be heard.

My breathing was extremely labored all the way to the safety vehicle and most of the way to the hospital. But by the time I was hospitalized, my breathing was back to normal and, except for the presence of some enzyme in my blood that indicated extensive destruction of muscle tissue, my tests showed no evidence of anything unexpected. I had a day in the hospital and most of a day at home to stew in my failure while the team hiked the relatively short distance to the coast at Laguna Verde and then paddled a rubber Zodiac boat an extremely long distance around the point at Playa Ancha back to the Reñaca beach at Viña where we had started four and a half days prior. I went and bought a bottle of champagne for the team and waited for them at the beach. They paddled through the plunging breakers and staggered ashore, pulling the boat onto the beach before hugging one another and rolling around in the sand like bear cubs. They were disqualified from being official finishers, but they were not denied the satisfaction of finishing. Margaret and I went over to them, popped the champagne, and poured them plastic cups, refilling them over and over until it was gone. I was proud of them, and yes, I felt terrible for failing them.

I'll never know what happened to me in the swim. It could be that the edema that had built up in my lower extremities started to be reabsorbed into my lungs in the cold water. It could have just been exhaustion. And I can't discount that it was panic, a totally mental breakdown, which would be surprising given all the hard things I had done in the water, including triathlon swims with packs of frantic swimmers and Marine Corps training in the cold, open ocean, in daylight and in darkness while loaded down with gear. Years later I read about a spate of deaths by drowning in triathlon competitions across the US. Many of the victims were strong swimmers who succumbed to panic attacks. Whatever it may have been, it marked my lowest point in Chile next to the house fire. My motivation was mismatched with guys trying to finish in as high a position as possible because I just wanted the experience of completing the event. They were competing for their professional reputations as commandos. I was a tourist.

And Carolina? What motivated her to compete so well? I don't know, but this event, in addition to being married for more than thirty years to a woman with a will and constitution of iron, firmly convinced me that the woman is the stronger being in the long run.

A year and a half later when we were getting ready to move back to the States, I heard a knock on the door one night about 8 p.m. Most of our household goods were packed and boxed up, ready to be moved. I thought it might have been the movers coming back to the house to pick up some tools. When I opened the door, there stood my Desafío teammates from eighteen months before with a bottle of champagne and a plaque they had made for me. The plaque has my name etched on it, and it includes the parachutist and commando insignias. The thought that they would go to that much trouble over a year later to say goodbye to a guy who had let them down is still astounding to me. It remains one of the classiest, most unselfish, and most thoughtful things anyone has ever done for me. We stood in my empty kitchen and toasted, raising plastic cups over and over until the champagne was gone, laughing and reliving our days of suffering together in the Chilean coastal hills. I soon got too emotional to speak.

As I write this, years hence, I am again overwhelmed.

With a ~~Pistol~~ Clipboard in His Hand

When Shakespeare wrote "Many wearing rapiers are afraid of those with goose quills,"[1] he was writing about actors and playwrights, but he may as well have been writing about unit leaders and peacetime exercise evaluators who carry a checklist for grading a unit's tactical capability. That evaluation process for Chilean Marine units, a near replica of what I had been through many times in US Marine units,[2] was familiar to me, and as the training officer for the destacamento, it fell to me to carry out a tactical evaluation of the rifle companies in the Batallón de Fusileros (Rifle Battalion). A rifle company consists of three rifle platoons and a weapons platoon, about 130 Marines in all, commanded by a *teniente primero* (equivalent to a US Marine captain). The idea was to put each company through a series of tasks involving amphibious assault, defense of an airfield, movement to contact, night attack, patrols, reaction to ambush, and finally, an attack with live ammo.

The amphibious assault was pretty low-budget and artificial, involving loading the rubber boats in the broad daylight at the yacht club in Concón and motoring across the bay to the Air Force base at Quintero. In spite of the basic nature of the evolution, it still forced the company commander to supervise ordering and preparing the gear, outfit everyone in life vests, waterproof all the gear, ensure that trained coxswains were driving the boats, and figure out who would load into which boats, which is harder than

---

1. William Shakespeare, *Hamlet*, Act 2, Scene 2.
2. Our process was called Marine Corps Combat Readiness Evaluation System (MCCRES). All our institutional acronyms were "MC" something, making them sound vaguely like menu items at a fast-food restaurant.

it sounds. You want to maintain unit integrity as much as possible, but you also want to spread the risk out in case a boat is hit by fire. In other words, you'd never want to put all your machine guns in the same boat, and you wouldn't want to have the unit commander and his executive officer (second-in-command) in the same boat or even near each other, but you want them close enough together to be able to quickly establish contact and work together once ashore. So the load plan always turns into a giant puzzle to solve to simply move from the ship to the beach, where you can start to fight back and not just be a target.

Once we got ashore at Quintero, the scenario changed to the defense of the airfield. The idea of the evaluation was to present the company staff with changing mission requirements and see how they adjusted, and how rapidly and effectively they evaluated their mission, formulated a plan, communicated that plan, and carried it out. The checklist I used to grade the company leadership included evaluating the actions and knowledge of the last rifleman in the last squad of the last platoon to test the effectiveness of communications and training. A Marine will always perform better when he or she knows the situation, the mission, and the plan. Conversely, a lack of knowledge engenders passivity, inactivity, and doubts about whether the leadership knows what it's doing. When a rifle company assumes a defensive position, you could be forgiven for thinking that they are in a period of rest. Nothing could be further from the truth. Every single Marine must start digging a protective position,[3] sectors of responsibility must be assigned, crew-served weapons must be emplaced to best protect the unit, and supplementary and alternative positions must be selected and prepared in case the unit is attacked from one of the flanks or the rear. Security patrols and listening/observation posts must be sent out, which necessitates the establishment and communication of procedures for departing and reentering friendly lines. Zones of dead space out beyond the unit's defensive line must be determined so they can be covered by indirect fire, and obstacles should be emplaced and

---

3. Soldiers in the US Civil War who had survived being on the receiving end of artillery would frantically dig in a defensive position using every conceivable tool, including the spoons and plates from their mess kits.

covered by fire. Supporting fires must also be integrated into the defense and requested from the unit that controls or coordinates the artillery and heavier mortars. As soon as the company went through the planning steps and had accomplished most of the steps of executing the defense, I'd call the aggressors (the commando unit that was part of the destacamento) to come dutifully attack the evaluated unit. Once the attack was over, I'd give the company commander a new mission, and the planning process would start for moving the company tactically to a location about ten miles inland for a night attack.

The entire evolution for just one company involved walking about forty-five to fifty kilometers over two nights and part of a day with minimal sleep. I had to do it for all three companies, so as soon as I wrapped up the exercise for one company, we'd re-set for another. The weeks I spent evaluating all three companies have blended into one sleep-deprived foggy memory, not just as I write this years later, but almost immediately after I did them. A few episodes still stand out in my memory, though.

Figure 5: Some of the best sleep I ever had was fifteen minutes at a time during short breaks after walking all night.

At one point while one of the companies was defending the airfield at Quintero, one of the earthquake tremors that routinely shake Chile occurred. Since we were outside in a wide-open space, I could see a ripple of earth from two hundred yards away that moved toward me from across the vacant airfield like a wave across the open ocean. That wave passed under the ammo can I was sitting on, nearly knocking me to the ground, and continued into the tree line to our front. It was the most surreal moment of earthquake tremors among the many I experienced in Chile.

One night as we hiked along a gravel country road between one attack and the next, a guy pulled up in a small car next to me, rolled down the window, leaned out, and asked me if I was the "jefe," only he pronounced it "shefe." Before I could explain that I was the controller (which I'm pretty sure would have meant nothing to him) and not the commander, he started yelling at me that he didn't want any of our troops coming to his house begging for food. The guy struggled to speak Spanish because he was French, and I know this doesn't speak well of me, but I found that enormously entertaining. He managed to make me understand that some soldiers had come to his home asking for food a couple of weeks before. Based on the timeframe, I knew there was no way our specific group of Marines had come to his house, and I tried to explain that to him, but he was determined to argue. The absurdity of the situation, an expat Frenchman in Chile thinking he's chewing out a Chilean Marine, who was in fact a US Marine with no command responsibility for the unit he was with, made me laugh, which only pissed the guy off more. His apoplectic anger, along with my laughing, made it hard for us to speak to and understand each other in our mutual second language, which would have made for a great Monty Python sketch. Finally, he rolled up his window and stomped on the gas of his four-cylinder Peugeot, and I saluted smartly in the darkness as he drove away.

The final night of the evaluation would have us establish a patrol base near the training area next to the destacamento. We'd try to let the guys get at least three or four hours of sleep there depending how fast they could hike to get there, because we wanted a reasonable amount of alertness for the final attack with live ammo. For me, sleep meant putting my sleeping bag inside a bivvy sack[4] and laying the whole package out on a thin padded mat that insulated my body from the cold ground. I'd then put my boots inside the bivvy but outside of the sleeping bag, get out of most of my clothes and push them down around the bottom of the sleeping bag where my feet would be, roll up a sweater for a pillow, climb inside the bag, and reach for the arms of Morpheus. One of the nights, though, it got so cold that we had to fold up our bivvy sacks the following morning by karate-chopping thin sheets of ice off of them. The company commander I was with, Favio Santibañez, joked that the whole thing was a dirty trick, that I should have advised him when I read him the tactical scenario that we had been supernaturally transported to Tierra del Fuego in winter.

At the end of one of the live fire exercises, there was an ugly incident involving a situation wherein a Marine was having trouble with his rifle, and his company commander loudly admonished him and ridiculed him for his indigenous name and heritage. The dynamics of race in Chile are broken down almost entirely along indigenous/non-indigenous lines. The Native Americans in Chile (primarily Mapuches) proudly claim to be the only indigenous people in Latin America not totally conquered by Imperial Spain or Portugal.[5] As Spanish colonial cities like Santiago and Valparaíso developed for Spanish colonists, large Native American populations continued to thrive in the south. To build a wall of European development between the capital and the Native American population in the south, the Chilean government invited German settlers to come and establish communities in places like Puerto Montt and Puerto Varas in the 1840s. The German influence is still seen in the names of people and places throughout Chile today. Prejudice against Native Americans in Chile is still strong enough that it is considered impolite to refer to anyone as

---

4. A bivvy sack made of waterproof but breathable GORE-TEX that encloses the entire sleeping bag, increases the sleeping bag's warming capability by about ten degrees, making a tent unnecessary in all but the harshest conditions.

5. The epic poem *La Araucana*, first published in 1569, details the Spanish conquest of Chile and pays homage to the ferocity and resilience of the Mapuche and Araucana people. The author, Alonso de Ercilla, was a Spanish soldier who took part in the conquest. He started composing the poem during breaks in the fighting.

indio or *indigena*. To say that someone is Native American, Chileans will call him or her an *Alemán de Temuco* (a German from Temuco).[6] It is unclear to me whether Chileans see themselves as racist, because the only time I remember the word *racismo* being used by Chileans was to describe white on black racism in the United States. One day when we were in the field, a US Marine sergeant, Brian Somers,[7] came over from the Marine School at Viña to work with the destacamento's snipers. During a break, one of the Chilean Marines pulled out a snack, the Chilean equivalent of a store-bought chocolate cupcake. Somers asked to see the wrapper and was astounded to see the brand name Negrita.[8] Somers told his Chilean counterpart that a product like that couldn't be sold in the US under that name because of the racial connotation. The Chilean, in an impressive feat of logical gymnastics, explained to the Chilean Marine next to him that the fact that snacks called Negrita can be sold in Chile without raising any eyebrows indicates that Chileans are much freer from racism than North Americans. I can tell you that when a US Navy carrier visited the port of Valparaíso and the US sailors went on liberty, the presence of a large contingent of black sailors caused quite a stir. I overheard one Chilean woman breathlessly tell a friend, "There are black people at the mall!" and they both broke into a trot to catch the next city bus there. I don't know if that kind of behavior is indicative of racism or curiosity, but to say "curious Chilean" is redundant. Perhaps because the population in Chile is so homogenous, anyone who looks different will be the target of long stares. Because Margaret was probably the tallest woman many Chileans had ever seen in person and she had the temerity to go shopping at the feria wearing her tennis gear, she was stared at a lot.

---

6. Temuco, the town in the south where the poet Pablo Neruda was born, is the epicenter of the Native American population in Chile.

7. Brian Somers performed superbly in his two-year assignment at the Chilean Marine School in Viña. He involved himself in every professional, social, and athletic event at the school and even went so far as to compete for the school judo team. I went to the Marine School gym to see him compete in a tournament in which the Marine School competed against the Chilean Army team. In one of the early matches, Somers absolutely flattened his opponent with a spectacular fall. The gym erupted into cheers the like of which I didn't hear the rest of the day. Somers was *their* teammate, and they loved seeing him do well.

8. *Negrita* could be applied to any small, black, feminine object, but the immediate uncontextualized translation to English would be something like "Little Blackie."

To carry a clipboard and follow a company is a process of evaluation, and you want it to be a process of teaching and coaching, too, but I can say in all honesty that the Chilean officers I served with in the destacamento generally knew how to do their jobs. The recommendations I had for them were fairly minor things (like reminding platoon leaders to ensure the Marines had their rifle sights adjusted to the distance for the sectors of fire they were assigned in the defense). The tips and suggestions I gave those who would listen were available to me because I was senior to the officers I was evaluating, I had combat experience, and I had operated in a wider variety of tactical scenarios and environments than they had, not because I was a US Marine and they were Chilean Marines. And I learned to never say, "In the US Marines we do it like this" (implying that they should copy us because we think we're better), because they would strongly resist that in spite of the fact that their doctrine was a faithful Spanish translation of ours. Their response would nearly always be, "But we don't have the same weapons systems and resources," which was a valid argument in some cases but was in many cases a cop-out.

The process of evaluation would sometimes teach me more about them than they realized. I was once tasked with evaluating the anti-aircraft machine gun section. The evaluation culminated with a live fire test in which the guns fired at hand-held flares that we shot into the sky. Of course, a bright flare drifting slowly in the sky is not exactly like an aircraft, but it is at least a target. I'd have to judge the effectiveness of fire based on seeing where the tracers (bullets that have a light chemical coating on the base that catch fire and illuminate in flight) flew in relation to the flare. Machine guns are not designed to be precision weapons, but one of the gunners, a young corporal, managed to actually cut the flare in half on two different targets, which to me was like two holes-in-one for a golfer in the same game. In the debrief after the evaluation, I specifically congratulated the corporal in front of the rest of the section for his precise firing. I said something like, "That was great firing, you should be a commando." An uncomfortable silence followed before someone else said, "But he doesn't know how to swim." Then another Marine said, "And he snores at night in the field." I realized, too late to do anything about it, that I had done that Marine no favors by bragging on him individually in front of everyone else. The social cohesion, hierarchy, and limits of individuality in Chile were vastly different from what I knew and experienced in the US Marines.

September 11: Theirs, Ours

Both years we were in Chile, the military units would have a ceremony commemorating the 1973 coup that put General Augusto Pinochet in power. The commemoration would be part of the daily formation on the parade ground, but we would wear our Alpha uniforms (theirs blue, mine green) and someone would read a short, militarized proclamation of the circumstances under Salvador Allende that made it necessary for the military to save the country (their words, not mine). Many books and documentary films have been written on the coup and the military government, so I won't rehash them here. I will tell you that I never knew a Chilean military officer who didn't seem to think the coup was the right thing to do[1] and that the military government was necessary for a time. They would say that, although some civilians were tortured and killed, it was not at Pinochet's bidding.[2] They would say that even though there was violence under the Pinochet regime, Pinochet didn't enrich himself from the treasury.[3] Most Chilean officers of my generation and older had a signed picture of Pinochet on the wall in their offices.

When we moved to Chile, I knew that the country had a socialist president, but I didn't know what the attitudes of the military were about the 1973 coup or about the administration in the year 2000. When I first heard the reading of this commemoration in September 2000, I had been in Chile for only a couple of months. I immediately started to wonder if the

---

1. Francisco Fierro told me about growing up as a middle-class kid in Santiago, having to stand in bread lines under the Allende government in the early 1970s.
2. This has been debunked.
3. This has also been debunked.

circumstances were in place for there to be another coup. I thought, "Well, this is interesting. If it happens, I'll have a front-row seat. I'll be kind of an eyewitness or subject matter expert among US Marines." I'm ashamed now of having been so nonchalant about the prospect, as irresponsible in my attitude as some bored sixth grader who hopes that a fight will break out in the lunchroom just to liven up the school day, but immensely more sociopathic. When I should have been praying that it would never happen again, I was casually indifferent about the possible repetition of a national horror in which over three thousand people, nearly all civilians, had been killed by their own countrymen with the tacit support and complicity of the United States.

Soon after I got to Chile, I quickly figured out a couple of things: President Ricardo Lagos was a socialist who had been forced into exile during the military regime ("As red as they come," a North American missionary friend told me), but his administration was, from all I could tell, the model of efficiency, hard work, and transparency. Even the most hardcore conservative would have to venture into tinfoil hat–wearing extremes to conjure up some reason to take up arms against the Chilean government in 2000. And although my military friends would never admit it to me, I think they realized that the coup isolated and penalized the country politically to such a degree and for such a long time that they'd never do it again. From 2000 until 2002, the Chilean military officers I knew were conservative but fairly apolitical. As another officer told me one day on the van coming home from work, "Nadie pesca."[4]

Our second September 11 in Chile was just a regular workday at the destacamento except for the commemorative reading at the morning formation. After the ceremony, I started walking back to quarters to change out of my Alpha uniform into camouflage utilities. A Marine from the headquarters ran up to me with a message from Comandante Wunderlich (who by this time was working in Valparaíso) to go watch the news on television. I went straight to the wardroom lounge and turned the TV to CNN en español. I think I got to the television just before the second plane hit, while the commentators were still wondering out loud if the first plane strike was an

---

4. This common Chilean phrase would be literally rendered into English as "No one fishes," but it means "No one pays attention, no one cares."

accident. Of course, the second plane striking the second tower cleared up all doubt. This was terrorism, plain and simple. It was just a question of who. I remember feeling numb seeing the buildings starting to catch fire, and I think I was completely horrified by the way both buildings collapsed into enormous clouds of ash, debris, and vaporized bodies. Television coverage soon shifted to the site of the crash into the Pentagon. I sensed that I was seeing something that marked an enormous change in the life of our country, and like a lot of US citizens abroad, I wondered how safe we were at that moment. The people at the Military Group in Santiago didn't know any more than I did. I called US Marine Forces South in Miami, and the only thing I got from the officer I talked to was a curt admonition for calling them on an unencrypted phone (as if I had access to any other kind of phone). I sat in front of the television for most of the rest of the workday as a few Chilean officers drifted in, watched for a few minutes, and left.

It turned out that Viña del Mar, Chile, may have been one of the safest places on the planet for a US citizen on 9/11. As the indications mounted that the attack was carried out by Muslim extremists operating out of Afghanistan, I started to prepare myself for immediate reassignment to an operational unit. To me, the only precedent for an attack like this was Pearl Harbor, and the war that followed mobilized seemingly every able-bodied man in the nation. I figured it would be a matter of days before I would be sent to an operational US Marine unit. I started researching and learning a few words in Pashto, and I sent an e-mail to my monitor[5] at Headquarters, Marine Corps, telling him I was available for reassignment. I didn't hear from him for months.

After I left Chile and moved to Miami, I heard a story about a small planning group made up of the five smartest majors and lieutenant colonels the Marine Corps could get its hands on. They worked in a small basement office at Headquarters, Marine Corps, in the Pentagon. This group's mission was to examine the strategic direction of the Marine Corps in broad terms so that the organization would be properly trained and equipped when called on. On that tragic day of September 11, just a couple of hours before

---

5. The monitor is the officer who assigns you to your next duty station.

the planes hit the towers and the Pentagon, the planning group was talking about where Marines would be expected to fight. They considered access to strategic resources, hotspots of ethnic strife, chokepoints in strategic lines of communication, and littoral proximity. Since the Marines can rapidly deploy to just about anywhere in the world on ships or in aircraft, the officer leading the discussion decided it would be easier to define where the Marine Corps *wouldn't* be likely to fight. He stood in front of a world map and waved his hand over a spot and said, "There, for instance. Right there. We would never be expected to fight there. It's landlocked and we have no strategic interests there." The place he was waving his hand over was Afghanistan, which turned out to be exactly where the country needed the Marines to fight in the weeks and months following 9/11. They got there by refueling CH-53 helicopters loaded with combat troops in flight, establishing an expeditionary airfield far inland, and landing C-130 cargo planes.

In Chile the 9/11 conspiracy theories flew thick and fast, the more preposterous the better. One was that the US government engineered the attack on ourselves so that we would have an excuse to wipe the map clean of all things Islamic and Middle Eastern. When a Chilean Marine Intelligence Officer (who was senior in rank to me) proposed that idea to me as we were riding the van home from the office at the end of a work day, I totally lost my composure and started yelling at the guy. My coming unglued caused great discomfort among the other officers in the van, and the guy kept saying over and over, "No te enojes conmigo" (Don't get mad at me). Another conspiracy theory was that, although we did not engineer or permit the attack, we knew exactly where Osama bin Laden was, and that we would pretend to not be able to find him until we had laid waste to the entire Islamic terrorist infrastructure.

Soon after the 9/11 attack, my number came up for promotion to lieutenant colonel. For US Marine officers, promotion is usually a low-impact event. You typically go into your commander's office, reaffirm the oath of office you took when you were commissioned, and the commander and another officer or possibly your spouse pins on your new rank insignia. But Comandante Del Real wanted to have a big ceremony. The destacamento's gringo was getting promoted in Chile, which was unprecedented.

An October ceremony was inconvenient because all their promotions are done en masse on January 1. The guy who was chief of staff of the Chilean Marine Corps at the time did all he could to diminish the ceremony. First he declared that Margaret could not be present at the promotion, which was a nonstarter for me. That edict was soon reversed. He then called my cell phone a few days before the promotion and told me that the ceremony would have to be canceled because my promotion warrant had been burned up in the attack on the Pentagon, which was false and an extremely tasteless joke. Despite his best efforts, the ceremony took place on October 1. The entire destacamento formed in dress blue uniforms. Comandante Wunderlich came from headquarters. The US military group commander and naval section chief came from Santiago and Valparaíso. The 1st Naval Zone band was bussed out from Valparaíso to play both national anthems. When the US flag was raised next to the Chilean one, all the emotions about the 9/11 attack that I didn't realize I had poured out of me. I wept like a grandmother. We had a nice reception at the cámara de oficiales afterward. It was a great day.

Figure 6: Promoted to lieutenant colonel in front of Destacamento Miller at Fuerte Aguayo near Concón, Chile, October 1, 2001.

Roughly concurrent with the 9/11 attack, an embarked US Marine UNITAS unit was set to visit the port of Valparaíso as part of their annual lap around South America. Because of the attack, they diverted south some 375 miles to Talcahuano, a smaller town where the port is a little more remote from the city. The plan was for us to do a big amphibious exercise together down south near Tierra del Fuego in October, and we were going to get together at the destacamento to do planning. But the reroute meant that I had to get on a plane, fly down there, and brief them on the plan. We went into the wardroom on the ship and I opened up the operations order written in Spanish and started to go through it with them in English, which was generally straightforward. I suppose that since the Romans conquered both the peninsula that later became Spain and the island that later became England, military language in Spanish and English is filled with cognates, words that are close together in form and meaning in both languages. But I got tripped up when I got to the fire support plan and started talking about the "initial point" where aircraft fly in tight circles and wait to receive close air support missions. The term in Spanish is *punto de espera* (waiting point, roughly). I guess I had worked so hard to learn the doctrinal term in Spanish, my brain intentionally filed away the English term in a locked vault and for the life of me, I couldn't remember it. I sat there with my mouth open, trying to access the little mental file drawer. The US Marines looked at me like, "That guy's been down here too long."

I was starting to suspect the same thing.

The Minister of Death

Near the close of every calendar year, the entire destacamento would go to the field together. At that point I would set aside my duties as training officer and evaluator for company-level combat evaluations and become the fire support coordinator. The fire support coordinator directs the business ends of mortars, artillery, naval gunfire, and airplanes against the enemy. Those weapons systems are, to a certain degree, indirect in that they involve the use of airspace as high-angle ordnance and are viewed and adjusted by an observer not collocated with the weapons systems doing the firing. Generally, those fires are much more effective when friendly units are in close proximity to the enemy and can close with them and exploit the temporary advantage afforded by the indirect fires. So, precise knowledge of where the good guys and bad guys are is crucial. Speed and accuracy count, too, because of the fluidity of actions on the battlefield. All of this may sound clinical and clean, but we're talking about hurling enormous explosive shells at other human beings to cause carnage obscene beyond belief. The training I received to "engage targets" conditioned me to think of my tasks in cold, impersonal terms, and that's how I tried to carry them out when I had to. It was always cleaner and easier when I knew noncombatants were not in the area. The enemy I was targeting was trying to do the same to me, and I was operating well within the laws of war. I confess that what I did in combat never cost me a minute of sleep, and I cheerfully practiced and taught the deadly doctrine of fire support coordination with the Chilean Marines as my language skills got better.

Going back to graduate school at Texas A&M in Hispanic studies after I retired from the Marines in 2005 changed my perspective about warfare a great deal. After making fast friends with international classmates, I realized that if in years prior there had just been a slight zig or zag in the geopolitical decision-making of their countries or mine, my Cuban and Colombian classmates and I might have faced each other in armed conflict. It should surprise no one that it turned out to be much more gratifying to study with, create alongside, and forge friendships with those people than to fight them. Texas A&M has a long history of training and preparing young people for military service. I was proud of that tradition even before I became a product of it. But when I returned to A&M for graduate studies, I was gratified to see that many of the classrooms in the Military Science Building were being used for non-military instruction. I even taught a couple of Spanish classes in there as a graduate student teacher. Cadets no longer marched to breakfast down the massive boulevard known as Military Walk that cuts through the heart of campus right in front of the old building where I took graduate seminars in Spanish with international students. To me, these were peace dividends, signs that we had won, at least the World Wars and the Cold War. I have read that John Adams, in a letter to his wife, wrote in 1780, "I must study politics and war, that our sons may have liberty to study mathematics and philosophy. Our sons ought to study mathematics and philosophy, geography, natural history and naval architecture, navigation, commerce and agriculture in order to give their children a right to study painting, poetry, music, architecture, statuary, tapestry and porcelain."[1] Although I believe in the value of military service and a reasonably robust armed forces, I strongly identify with Adams's statement. My own sons studied film and philosophy in college, and although I would have been fine with either of them serving in the military, I'm glad they didn't have to.

When I had been with the destacamento for only a few months and Walter Wunderlich was the comandante, we went to the area near our headquarters for a couple of weeks of training. Actually, we trained for about ten

---

1. John Adams, "Letters of John Adams, Addressed to His Wife," January, 1841, https://www.goodreads.com/work/quotes/6405193.

days and then underwent a combat readiness evaluation conducted by officers from the headquarters in Valparaíso. Wunderlich surprised me by ordering the destacamento headquarters to be completely emptied out and sent to the field. That meant that every nurse, every breadmaker, and every bean counter was taken from their permanent workspaces and put in the field, where they resumed their duties under canvas. He even had the sick people taken out of the infirmary and placed in a field hospital. As extreme as those measures sounded at the time, I came to totally understand them. Wunderlich was no fool. He knew that if he didn't hold a hard line, he'd look up on the second day of training and half the headquarters company would be back in the relative comfort of the permanent buildings two or three miles away "attending to things."

One of the features of field training when the whole destacamento went out was that the officers on the staff all ate dinner together in a tent with a table, camp chairs, and lanterns. We'd go through the chow line with our mess kits and canteen cups with everyone else, but then we'd enter this tent with the seven or eight other staff officers. It was essentially the comandante's personal dining tent, and we staff officers were the permanently invited guests. Anyone else who needed to come in would reach through the tent flap, knock on the wooden tentpole, and say, "Con permiso," before sticking his head in to state his business. We'd eat and then, characteristic of the *sobremesa* one would experience anywhere in the Spanish-speaking world, spend at least an hour in there talking about everything imaginable with Wunderlich holding court. Wunderlich was opinionated, well-read, and highly intelligent, and he would make efforts to include me in the discussion. I was getting much better at being able to participate conversationally. I even had a breakthrough when I overheard a long phrase that was composed entirely of Chilean Navy slang and casual profanity and realized that I understood it all. But by ten o'clock at night, at the end of a long day of working and socializing entirely in Spanish, I would be mentally exhausted. This training took place right around the time of the contested presidential election of 2000. The comandante asked me to explain the electoral college and then explain the glitches in that specific election, the hanging chads and whatnot. I don't know that I would have done a great job in English, but my explanation was truly sketchy in Spanish. When I finished, Wunderlich asked reprovingly, "Aren't you the guys who go around to other countries certifying *their* elections?"

The group in the command-post dining tent was comprised mostly of senior officers, but one of us was a young subteniente, Rodrigo Pávez. At Wunderlich's prompting, Pávez was explaining all the nicknames of the subtenientes in the destacamento. Pávez's nickname, Mono (monkey), was practically inherited because his father, also a Marine officer, was nicknamed Mono Pávez.[2] One of Subteniente Pávez's classmates, Hugo Huerta, had been awarded the nickname of *Cabeza de maní* (Peanut head), but repeatedly tried to make up his own, unsuccessfully trying to replace Peanut head with ones having to do with motorcycles, being tall, and Marlboro cigarettes. Of course, the rules of nicknames are international and universal. You don't get to choose your own, and the less you like the one you get, the more firmly it sticks. We were still chuckling over this story when someone came rapping at the tentpole. "Adelante," said Comandante Wunderlich. As if on cue, a head tentatively entered the tent flap. It belonged to Hugo Huerta, the very peanut himself. We nearly fell out of our chairs. Before Huerta could state his business, Wunderlich asked, "Hey, what's your nickname?" as if he were benignly curious. Huerta responded, "Um . . . Moto." "No!" shot back Wunderlich, smiling triumphantly and wagging his index finger, "Cabeza de maní." Huerta shot an incredulous look at the traitor Pávez. I'm not sure Huerta ever took care of the business for which he had come to the dining tent in the first place, but he later exacted his revenge by writing a song entitled "Mala suerte tiene Mono Pávez" (Monkey Pávez has Bad Luck), which he performed with gusto at unit parties.

Working in the command post meant standing watch, and we all took late-night shifts monitoring radios and generally being bored and sleepy. As

---

2. In an episode famous throughout the Chilean Marine Corps, one Saturday morning in Viña, Mono Pávez Sr. went out for a jog around the neighborhood with his dog. Someone driving past rolled down his car window and yelled, "Hey, dog, where are you going with that monkey?"

often as not, my partner on watch was Suboficial Castro. About twenty-five years of enlisted service was required to make suboficial, the equivalent of first sergeant in the US Armed Forces. Castro was the operations chief, the senior enlisted man in the operations section. Like a lot of senior enlisted men in all services, he seemed to know everything and know how to do everything. Castro is permanently sunburned and skinny, as if he were constructed of articulated beef jerky. He either had a body double or he never actually slept because every time I was in the command post he was already in there. I had a hard time understanding him at first because he spoke through his teeth like a ventriloquist and he was a *huaso*[3] from the country. He was a tremendous help to me the whole time I was in the destacamento. In later years he served as the suboficial mayor of the whole Chilean Marine Corps, an honor richly deserved.

Near the end of our evaluation that first year we got word that the hot water had been turned off back at the destacamento due to repairs. Filthy from two weeks in the field with camouflage paint all over my face, ears, and neck, I took this as awful news. I remember hearing it when I was standing next to Francisco Fierro and Comandante Longhi, the second-in-command of the destacamento. I said to them that that situation was a *pico en el ojo*.[4] Longhi, surprised that I knew this pithy phrase, remarked that my Chileanization was well underway.

By the time the destacamento went through the evaluation process again a year later, I was much more seasoned and we had a whole different crew on the staff. The timeless Suboficial Castro was still there, but Cristián del Real was the comandante, Roberto Opazo the segundo comandante. The new operations officer was David Hardy, a great Chilean name. Hardy is the son of British immigrants. His grandfather had been an officer in a Gurkha regiment in World War II. David and I were the same rank when we worked together, and he was already a legend in the Chilean Marine Corps

---

3. The Chilean huaso is the equivalent of the North American cowboy or the Argentine gaucho. The standard huaso dress is a flat, black, broadbrimmed hat, a brightly colored wool poncho, and enormous spurs.

4. A literal translation would be "A beak in the eye," but in Chile *pico* is a euphemism for "penis." This phrase would not be uttered in polite company but was common among Marines as a metaphor for an extremely disagreeable experience.

for having survived a total parachute malfunction as a young lieutenant. His parachute never deployed on a free fall jump, and he only survived because he fell into a stand of eucalyptus trees, the branches of which decelerated his fall. He spent a year in the hospital, where his shattered lower leg bones were rebuilt with a paste made of cow bones and some of his own hip bone. Years after, when I knew him, he could not run but could walk and even hike long distances with no problem. He seemed to suffer no psychological effects from the accident. He told me that he would even parachute again if he ever got the green light from the doctors. About a year before coming to the destacamento to be the operations officer, Hardy made a name for himself again with a feat of intellect that may have been as astounding as his partial win over terminal velocity: he graduated first in his class from the Escuela de Guerra Naval.[5]

Escuela de Guerra is an exceptionally challenging course due to the massive amount of material that must be read, analyzed, and written about. Students and instructors alike often spend all night reading and writing. For that year, they become strangers to their families and put on fifteen to twenty pounds of body fat. What was remarkable about David Hardy's feat was that he is a Marine and not an executive branch (that is to say, ship-driving Navy) officer. Remember, seniority in the Chilean Navy means everything, and because of that, Marines, along with supply officers and Coast Guard officers, were required to sit in the back of the classroom. You don't have to be an expert in pedagogy to know that sitting near the front of the class is better for learning, and you could imagine that Escuela de Guerra Naval was a ship-centric course where a Marine would be at a disadvantage. But David Hardy overcame both of those limitations. It wasn't easy, though. He and a Navy guy were neck and neck throughout the whole course. The evening they both turned in their final papers, neither knew who would come out as the honor graduate at the next day's ceremony. They exited the classroom about the same time and agreed to go have a beer to celebrate the end of the grueling year. They went to a bar, relaxed and had a drink, and went home to get some sleep. David arrived

---

5. The Chilean equivalent of Naval War College. Officers attend this course when they've already had about 18–20 years of service.

for graduation the next day and was shocked to hear that his classmate had died of a massive heart attack in his sleep. Hardy graduated number one in his class, a feat no other Marine had ever achieved and which I doubt has been replicated since.

As a prize for graduating first in his class, David was sent to Buenos Aires, Argentina, to go through the Argentinian Navy version of the exact same course the following year. You read that right. I cannot for the life of me see how this was a good deal. It's like the winner of a blueberry pie–eating contest being awarded a blueberry pie. But Hardy dutifully went, glad for the opportunity to represent his country. While driving with his family to and from Buenos Aires at the beginning and end of the year, he was pulled over on the highway by Argentine police and required to pay bribes.

David Hardy wore his considerable renown lightly, being an incredibly friendly, patient guy. He was without pretense or arrogance, and he loved being a Marine. We worked together frequently in the office, but when we were in the field we were almost joined at the hip. We opted not to bring tents to the field since the weather was nice, and at night when we weren't training or on watch we'd just roll out our sleeping bags next to the command post somewhere where we wouldn't be stepped on or run over by a vehicle. In the mornings I was able to witness his elaborate routine of loosening up his damaged feet and ankles just so he could get up and walk around.

Because much of the staff had turned over since the previous year and my language skills had improved, I was an element of continuity since I remembered what had and hadn't worked in the evaluation the year before. In the command post my map board was between those of the operations officer and the intelligence officer, where I could immediately do targeting based on enemy and friendly positions. The firing agency representatives from mortars and artillery were just on the other side of a little window that separated us from the back of a vehicle that formed the back wall of the mobile command post. So I was constantly coordinating, verifying, planning, and questioning. It was hard but it was fun to be totally involved.

Figure 7: With Comandante Del Real training in the desert near Caleta Cifuncho, Chile, in 2001.

Intently focused on improving the unit's tactical capability, Comandante Del Real's pet peeve was camouflage, so he would demand that everyone put the camouflage paint on their faces as soon as they were standing on the dirt of the training area. A Marine's enthusiasm for putting on camouflage paint is inversely proportional to the years of service, probably because new guys put it on so poorly, just around the face as if it were a mask. To do it right, you've got to paint your neck all the way down to your t-shirt, your eyelids, your forehead up to the hairline, your ears, *in* your ears, and on the sides and back of your head if your hair is short enough. And it's a bear to take off. It never failed that you would be sitting in church three days after you thought you were clean, only to hear your wife whisper that you still had green paint in your ear. Interestingly enough, I rarely saw Del Real with camouflage paint on his own face. Even though he was liked and respected, the paradox of his hard line on everyone cammying up and his own aversion to putting it on himself was a running joke in the unit. It's natural, I guess, that Marines think of the comandante as a guy having an easy job and enjoying immense privilege, which must have given rise to the famous "siempre quise ser comandante" (I always wanted to be a commander) story. It was told to me by a couple of different guys, but I had the best version from Favio Santibañez, a former professional soccer player who was a company commander in the destacamento when I knew him. As it goes, there was a Navy officer named Sánchez who never got promoted high enough to be a comandante and ended up retiring at the rank far inferior to those of his classmates who continued in service. Embittered at never making comandante and being sent into involuntary retirement, he spent nearly all his savings buying the exact same type of sedan that was issued to commanders and renting an office in Valparaíso near the Chilean Navy Headquarters. With what was left of his money he hired a couple of former Navy enlisted guys to be his driver and his secretary. Sánchez paid the driver to come by his house, pick him up, and drive him to work while he read the paper in the back seat like he imagined all the comandantes do. When he got to his office every morning, he had trained his secretary to come in, give him a folder full of papers, and tell him they needed his urgent attention. He ignored them and kept reading the paper, as he imagined the comandante would do. About noon, he'd wander down to the Navy Club for lunch. After dining, he'd be a little sleepy, so he'd nap most of the afternoon, just like he assumed the comandante always did. At about 5 p.m., his driver would park out front to take him home. Just as Sánchez was climbing into the back seat of the car, his secretary was obliged to rush out of the office with a stack of papers, which he would present to the fake "comandante," saying, "The admiral says these reports must be submitted before you can leave today." All that expense, all that pretense, was put together so that Sánchez could say with relish, "Tell the admiral to stick it in his ass."

To the South on the Aquiles

Since Thanksgiving is a US-specific holiday, it should surprise no one that it's not celebrated in Chile. Christmas is not a real big deal, either, but in the January/February timeframe, in the style of Italians in August, it seems like everyone in Chile takes an entire month off. And off means off. I saw Chilean Marines go into total relax mode and grow full beards during their month off without fear of recriminations or repercussions. The month-long vacation in Chile is a family affair, and when we were there it seemed to be intentionally low-tech and remote.[1] A common vacation in Chile would be to go to a cabin on a lake somewhere in the south (the vacation timeframe was most promising for good weather in the south of Chile), take walks, play cards and board games day in and day out, and spend all your waking hours together as a family.

We wanted to visit our friends the Fierros in Punta Arenas and see Patagonia, so at the suggestion of our Chilean Navy and Marine friends, we requested to embark on the Aquiles, a Chilean Navy vessel, for the ship's annual trip to Punta Arenas, the southernmost Chilean city that overlooks the Straits of Magellan. As a cost-saving measure for the Navy, the Aquiles transported families and their household goods from duty stations in the North to the South (and vice versa), and anyone else holding a Chilean Navy ID card who wanted to travel on the ship could go space-available

---

1. The notable exception is the once-in-a-lifetime trip to Disney World. Chileans will scrimp and save for many years for a trip to Florida to see "Ratón Mickey." For years hence, other Chileans will speak of the Disney-goers with hushed reverence, as if they had been raptured to heaven for a ten-day period.

and pay a fee that covered their meals.[2] When we initially contacted Chilean Navy Headquarters about traveling on the Aquiles, they quoted us a price four or five times higher than what our friends told us it would be. A couple more phone calls and some documentation were required to convince them that we were not short-term visitors or US embassy employees, but that I was a member of a Chilean operational unit. We ran into that phenomenon occasionally, being charged the "gringo price" for something until Chileans who knew us could vouch for us and prove that we deserved to pay what the Chilean Navy families were paying.

In February 2002, just about the warmest part of southern hemisphere summer, we boarded the Aquiles in Valparaíso, excited to be going on such a unique trip. Margaret packed special travel bags for the boys with books, activities, and Harry Potter–themed toothbrushes. The Aquiles was something of a showpiece for the Chilean Navy, built and decorated to host presidential visits and transport VIPs. The ubiquitous Navy gray paint was covered up with wood paneling, and some of the narrow, steep ladders had been replaced with wide stairwells. The *salón de estar* (lounge) was spacious and featured large windows. We ate at small round tables in the officers' mess, nearly always with people we didn't know. Whether we sat with people twenty years older or twenty years younger than us, Chileans conversed as freely with us as they would with old friends.

Our stateroom had two sets of bunk beds with plenty of closet space and a bathroom with shower, sink, and mirror. I've never seen the inside of a cruise ship, so I don't know how it would compare, but it was plenty nice enough for us. Soon after we sailed from Valparaíso and headed south in the open seas, we got into a little bit of rough water and Margaret and the boys got seasick. If they were in bed and horizontal, they handled it pretty well, but as soon as they got up, one would throw up, immediately followed by the other. Even getting them upright long enough to get their pajamas on them would make them seasick, and they even threw up once while brushing their teeth. "I never imagined that Harry Potter toothbrushes would have that effect on kids!" I exclaimed. "Daaaaaaad!" they wailed with

---

2. The vacation season in Chile roughly corresponded with the new calendar year when Permanent Change of Station (PCS) moves were made.

a mixture of misery and the suppressed laughter that constitutes the natural response to dad humor.

After five days underway and short stops in Talcahuano and Puerto Montt, we pulled up to the pier in Punta Arenas, where a small waddle of penguins formed an unofficial welcoming committee. We arrived in the broad daylight of 6:30 p.m. on the 17th of February, a date and time commemorated on a beautiful chart given to us by the ship's captain, Matías Purcell Echeverría. Purcell was a nice guy and a good leader who figured into an episode at the end of the last big exercise I did with the Chilean Navy and Marines a few months later. He commanded one of the naval units in the Chilean phase of the multinational UNITAS exercise that included our destacamento. At the end of the exercise debrief in the port of Valparaíso, he and one of the senior US Navy representatives ceremonially exchanged gifts, which is customary. The rep from US Navy South Headquarters in Mayport, Florida, a US Navy commander, got up and made a long speech in English about how much he enjoyed working with "Captain Echeverría." He went so far as to say that he felt like he and "Captain Echeverría" were brothers for life from that point forward. He eventually handed over the commemorative plaque to Captain Purcell and sat down, satisfied with himself, oblivious to the fact that he was committing a big cultural faux pas by referring to the man by only his maternal last name, the cultural linguistic equivalent of walking around with an eight-foot section of toilet paper stuck to your shoe. You would typically refer to someone in that situation with their rank and paternal last name ("Purcell" in this case), or if you wanted to be formal or prevent possible confusion between two people with the same paternal last name you could use both last names together. It was a scene I saw a few times in Chile: an official from the US with a lot of political capital, but without enough language capability or cultural understanding to properly employ it.

The Fierros picked us up at the pier and took us to their home. We enjoyed their hospitality and caught up with what had happened in both of our families since they had left Viña the year before. Francisco took us over to the destacamento, where he was second-in-command, for a nice meal and visit. The segundo comandante job at Punta Arenas was good for

Francisco's career, but it was a tough place to live. The winters were brutally long, dark, and cold, the wind howled year-round,[3] and if you had family in Santiago, you were a thirty-six-hour drive (most of it through Argentina) or an expensive plane ticket away from them. But the demands of living in such a difficult place produced a tight social network, and whenever we had a Chilean Marine Corps anniversary celebration in Viña where we sang the hymns of all the destacamentos, the song of the Punta Arenas unit was sung with the most volume and enthusiasm.

Touring around Punta Arenas included an obligatory visit to the downtown plaza. In the center of the plaza there's a large monument topped by a statue of Ferdinand Magellan. Arrayed around the lower level are bronze statues of Indians. The bare foot of one of the Indians hangs about chest high from the ground, and legend has it that if you rub the Indian's big toe, you are destined to return to Punta Arenas. Dani or Franciquito explained this custom to our boys, and as they ran toward the statue, Cucky Fierro yelled "Nooooo!" in mock horror at the prospect of returning to Punta Arenas. We rented a car in Punta Arenas for the drive up to Torres del Paine in Chilean Patagonia. We passed through the cool little town of Puerto Natales, where we had lunch before continuing north into Patagonia. The need to buy gas soon presented itself, and we started to get a little nervous in that unpopulated place until we finally saw a tiny building with *gasolina 93* painted on the side. It turned out that the gas pump was inside the little building where they sold 93-octane gas *sin plomo* (unleaded). While we were refueling, a nice German couple pulled up on matching BMW motorcycles. The man explained that they were riding the length of South America, apparently without showering.

During the seventy-mile drive from Puerto Natales to Torres del Paine, the two-lane paved road turned gravel, and we eventually arrived at the park without realizing it. There was understandably no fence of any type, and the entrance and headquarters were hardly recognizable as such. Although it was a little unsettling to be constantly checking the map

---

3. There's a *Monumento al viento* (Monument to the Wind) just outside the Punta Arenas city limits along the highway, and the walls of buildings downtown are outfitted with ropes for handholds to get around windy corners.

and asking ourselves if we were in the right place, it was delectable to be in a world-famous national park (a protected World Biosphere Reserve, actually) in a natural, pristine place free from crowds, advertisements, and directional signage. Having grown up going on vacations in the US to the Smoky Mountains where the dueling tourist traps of Rock City and Ruby Falls seemed to be in competition for who could put out more trashy signage per highway mile, we found the unspoiled beauty of Torres del Paine refreshing. At the entrance we went into the headquarters to register and pay our entrance fee. While perusing a poster on the wall that depicted the different species that made up the park's wildlife, I stopped a passing park ranger, nodded to the poster, and asked, "So, are these animals we're seeing near the headquarters *guanacos* or llamas?" The park ranger answered with characteristic Chilean evasiveness, "This poster was produced at the national headquarters in Santiago." I suppressed a grin and said, "I see." Then I asked him, "Are there trout in the rivers and streams in the park?" He responded, "Fishing in the park is prohibited." I thanked him for his time and went to find my family. By then I had learned to accept that those were honest Chilean answers: not what I wanted to know, but rather, what he wanted me to know.

We drove to a resort in the park where we had reservations. In the large dining room, I heard many Asian and European languages as well as Spanish, but no English. Our first morning at the resort we went out on a guided horseback tour. We each had our own horse, except for Jackson, who rode in my lap. The mountainous centerpiece of the park, the Cordillera del Paine, was in sight the whole time we rode, and the trails took us through valleys, around lakes, and within sight of glaciers. We alternately experienced sunshine, light rain, and intermittent snow during our three-hour ride. *Paine*, the word that gives the park its name, means "blue" in the Tehuelche language, but to me the dominant colors were the green of the evergreens and fescues, the bright red wildflowers, and the yellowish-brown Darwin's slipper. That night, the winds howled with enough force to keep us awake in our comfortable room, and I was sure that anyone camping in the park trying to stay in a tent was struggling to keep from blowing away like a tumbleweed.

The next day we checked the boys in with a babysitter and hiked up to the famous *torres* (towers), the famous rock pillars adjacent to the *cuernos* (horns) that are so picturesque, you can be assured that you've seen pictures of them in outdoor sports magazines and car ads. The last few hundred meters up to the torres required going up a steep boulder field, sometimes scrambling with the aid of the hands. The long hike was well worth the view, and we returned to the resort tired and happy. The next day was dedicated to the drive back to Punta Arenas after a drive around the southern side of the cuernos, where we crossed paths with hikers and bikepackers.

Since the Aquiles had long sailed from Punta Arenas back to the north, our return trip was a three-and-a-half-hour flight from Punta Arenas to Santiago on the outstanding national airline LanChile.[4] Another shuttle ride back to Viña from Santiago and we were finally back home.

---

4. LanChile has since been subsumed by LATAM Airlines.

On How Things Can
Always Get Worse

In April of 2002, Destacamento Miller had a chance to send a task force of about 150 Marines to the south of Chile for amphibious and riverine training. The concept entailed boarding one of the amphibious ships and sailing south from Valparaíso for several days to get down past Puerto Cisnes for a night rubber boat landing at a little town with the fabulous name of Puyuhuapi. At first light, we'd hike about fifty kilometers to the town of La Junta on the Palena River. The next day, we'd traverse down the river to its mouth at Puerto Marín Balmaceda and eventually re-embark by climbing up the wet nets at sea just off the coast.

Our task force was commanded by Capitán de Corbeta Patricio Silva, a Northern European–looking guy with wavy, graying hair. Patricio's name was logically shortened to the nickname of *Pato*, which also means "duck" in Spanish. In most places in Latin America, *pato* also means "gay man," but Chile was not one of those places, so most guys named Patricio were called Pato in Chile. Silva had attended a year-long US Marine Corps school for captains called Amphibious Warfare School. He was steeped in US Marine doctrine, and I think he had a good command of English, although he and I always spoke Spanish. I liked and respected him. He had successfully completed commando training when he was younger and was a tough guy. One weekend during his year in Quantico, Virginia, he ran a fifty-mile trail race, essentially two back-to-back running marathons on a difficult course, without any special preparation. His toughness extended to the way he dealt with subordinates. He often spoke to them with a harshness that made me wince, and I myself was not exactly the paragon of niceness with my Marines during much of my career, especially when I was in combat arms units.

At the port in Valparaíso we boarded the *Rancagua*, a carbon copy of the *Chacabuco*, the ship on which I embarked to do my first mission with the Chilean Marines. The *Rancagua* was captained at that time by Comandante Charlie Zavala, a compact, balding guy with glasses. Zavala was a live wire, a gregarious, outlandish, funny guy who was famous in the Chilean Navy for the way he partially completed Chilean SEAL training back when he was a new subteniente. The Chilean Navy's version of SEALs was called the *Buzos Tácticos* (Tactical Divers) and their yearlong training was, as you might imagine, supremely difficult, with a high rate of attrition. Near the end of his course, Zavala was one of the few officers who had not washed out of training. When they went for final physical examinations, Charlie Zavala was found to have eyesight sufficiently bad enough to disqualify him from being a Buzo Táctico. He was told he'd be immediately dis-enrolled and sent back to the ship-driving officer training pipeline. I don't know why you would need better vision to see underwater, where you can't see anything anyway, than to see the buoys and markers and signals necessary to drive a ship. Zavala successfully begged not to be dropped from the Buzos Tácticos course, a concession he knew would condemn him to undergo some of the most challenging training of his life without the possibility of graduating. Whether it was for his reputation or his own personal satisfaction, he didn't want to fail, even due to medical circumstances that were no fault of his own.

Charlie Zavala kindly hosted me for dinner in his stateroom[1] the first night we were aboard. Traditionally, having an officer from another country on board a navy ship in any country is a big deal. There is even a proscribed ceremonial procedure (that I always messed up) for requesting to come aboard as a foreign officer. Your presence is announced over the intercom to the whole ship, achieving the dual purpose of politely rendering honors and letting your own sailors know to hide the classified material. Since I was in Destacamento Miller, I usually boarded and disembarked with the Chilean Marines and without ceremony. The ship's captain would usually either

---

1. The ship's captain does not usually eat in the wardroom with the other officers.

minimally acknowledge me or ignore me altogether. This was fine with me since I had no insightful pointers to share about ships' captaincy, and I always figured he had plenty to do without chatting me up. But Zavala was particularly outgoing and engaging. As we dined, we talked about a range of subjects, and I remember his vivid assessment of Chilean behavior at soccer matches. "We're polite, well-mannered people, right?" he said. "But what happens when we go to a soccer match and the referee walks out? The match hasn't even started, and we start screaming *conchasumadre*[2] at the guy." I've ruminated on the point I believe he was making and I believe that his observation points to a phenomenon of equilibrium in human behavior. Chile has always been conservative and Catholic, perhaps not great environments for freely expressing oneself in conventional terms, which I believe may explain the enormous amount of graffiti in Chile and other Latin American countries. If you have no other recourse for expression, you might grab a can of spray paint and risk scrambling over a busy highway in the dark of night to write "Capitalism is Death" in letters as tall as you are. So, there are balanced extremes of controlled and uncontrolled messaging in Chile. And there are balanced extremes of politeness and incivility. When you ride the city bus in Santiago, an enormous, bustling city where everyone is in a hurry, it is common for ten people to get off at a bus stop and each and every one of them pause to thank the bus driver, but once enclosed in the privacy and autonomy of their own cars people drive as if they are on a personal mission to inconvenience every other driver on the road. You don't dare signal your intention to change lanes while driving on a Santiago freeway because the driver in that lane a hundred feet back will gallop up and pass you as if to say, "Nope, you can't have my spot." It's as if since cars didn't exist in sixteenth-century Spain, the courtly manners devised for people standing upright could not be applied to people sitting in a car. And Chileans, who are unfailingly polite, considerate, and respectful, will go to a soccer match and unleash a torrent of profanity for three hours that strains the limits of sexual and geometric possibility.[3] Maybe that's what restores the balance. We call some guy a *sacoweas* (nutsack) at the top of our

---

2. This Chilean insult can only be faithfully translated into English as "motherfucker."
3. I know the same thing happens at NFL and college football games in the US, but we North Americans are not unfailingly polite, considerate, and respectful the rest of the week.

lungs for an entire Saturday afternoon so that we can be models of cordiality the other six and a half days of the week.

The environment on the *Rancagua* was congenial and social. One of the ways to describe the type of ship the *Rancagua* is would be to employ the designation *barcaza*, the Spanish word for "barge." But the ship's segundo comandante, on the third night in a row of us drinking pisco sours[4] in the officers' mess, told me his own twist on the term, explaining, "Es tu bar. Es tu casa. Es tu barcasa."[5]

Unlike most US and Chilean ship-driving Navy guys who view land only as a hazard to navigation, Comandante Zavala reveled in the details of what our detachment would do ashore. Even though no aircraft or live ammo was involved in this operation, there was a fair amount of risk to life and limb and he wanted to make sure it went well. We had a plan to use high-frequency radios to maintain communications with the ship at different stages of the exercise in case of an emergency. To load the Marines on rubber boats via wet nets at night in the open sea is inherently dangerous. It was not unheard of for a Marine to lose his grip on the nets and fall, loaded down with pack and rifle, between the ship and the rubber boat. The night amphibious assault was no sure thing, either. Boats can run into one another, Marines can fall overboard during rapid maneuvering, and high surf can flip loaded boats. Additionally, the weather in the south of Chile at that time of year is fearsomely windy and rainy. The Chilean Marines like to say that there's no point in using the phrase *mal clima* to describe the weather in the south. All you have to say is southern weather. It will be understood to be cold and rainy.

First, we offloaded three pickup trucks at Puerto Cisnes, a tactical artificiality, but the only reasonable way to get the Zodiac boats and engines to the town of La Junta, where the *carretera austral* (southern highway)

---

4. Pisco, a powerfully strong, clear brandy, is the national drink of both Chile and Perú, and people from both countries argue about which nation makes the best pisco sour (pisco with egg white, lime juice, and simple syrup). The mix of pisco and some variety of cola (piscola) is a favorite of Chilean Marines. The destacamento's subtenientes would occasionally contest for the title of best *piscolero*, the guy who could drink the most piscola the fastest.

5. In Latin American Spanish, *s* and *z* are pronounced the same, so the linguistic joke "barcaza-barcasa" works perfectly.

crossed the Palena River. After a harrowing night amphibious-landing in the driving rain adjacent to the little coastal town of Puyuhuapi, we slept under ponchos and tarps for about an hour before the sun came up. When daylight came, we put on our packs in a steady drizzle of rain and formed parallel lines on either side of the carretera austral, which is an inarguable achievement of the Pinochet regime, a tangible sign of the government's commitment to expand infrastructure and services to far-flung, lightly populated parts of the country. Anyone could cynically suspect that the regime only wanted to connect the south of the country with the rest of it for military purposes, but anyone who has seen firsthand the relative neglect with which national governments in Latin America treat their outlying areas would appreciate the effort that the Chilean government, now democratic (socialist, in fact, when we were there), dedicated to extend governance into the far-flung and lightly populated parts of the country. I saw this phenomenon all over Chile: good roads, tunnels and bridges, and governmental presence in even the most lightly populated and far-flung locations. The word "carretera" communicates the idea of a highway, but this far south, the carretera austral was a two-lane gravel road, well-maintained and perfectly trafficable.

The rain would occasionally slacken or intensify, but never went away while we hiked through the day. The wind continued to blow the rain sideways and ensured a constantly low-effective wind-chill. My great error was bringing only a poncho instead of the GORE-TEX suit that would have kept me much dryer and warmer. I reasoned that it would stop raining eventually and that I'd just wear my wet clothes dry at some point in the day. I was wrong. We adopted the time-honored system of hiking for fifty minutes and resting for ten, but it was too cold for us to want to stop for very long. We even skipped any kind of a lunch break. The scenery was an uninterrupted series of varying shades of lush green with occasional slim waterfalls. The sound of falling water, whether it be from waterfalls or rain hitting our helmets, was accompanied by footfalls on gravel, squeaking packstraps under load, and the rattle of carried weapons being adjusted. We rarely encountered vehicular traffic. Along the roads there were a few small, simple homes with ample gardens and a handful of sheep or cattle.

The standard attire for everyone who lived in that region consisted of wool sweaters and rubber boots. We covered the fifty kilometers in about twelve hours, not terribly fast, and by the end of the hike, as the sun started to set, I was feeling the effects of being in the cold rain and wind all day much more than the effort of walking.

As we neared La Junta, I overheard one of the truck drivers tell someone that a *galpón* had been found for us to spend the night in, which made me unreasonably happy. A galpón is a warehouse, and I was imagining something well-lighted and windproof with a dry, level floor. It turns out what they were calling a galpón was a dairy barn. To get to it from the road we sloshed through about eighty yards of ankle-deep mud. I didn't care, though, since it was infinitely better than spending a second consecutive night trying to sleep in the cold rain. Once inside, the Marines staked out places among the hay bales and stalls, got out of their wet uniforms and donned warm clothing to sleep in, and pulled out cigarettes, entire cakes, bottles of pisco, and who knows what all else. I rolled out my sleeping mat and bag next to Pato Silva while we all stood around sharing food and stories of how the previous night and day had gone. An hour after getting into the barn, I was still freezing, so I climbed into my sleeping bag. As any winter camper knows, a sleeping bag doesn't make you warm; your body heat makes the bag warm, so it takes a while in the bag to start to feel the sensation of warmth. As I was lying there shivering, a young Marine, probably a conscript, was wandering around asking if anyone had seen his pack. I felt bad for the kid and wondered why his squad leader or platoon sergeant wasn't helping him. After about the third lap of this kid wandering by asking about his pack, Pato Silva, commander of the whole task force, the guy who always seemed to be the toughest on the Marines, got out of his sleeping bag, pulled on his boots, and without complaining or griping at the kid, went and helped him find his pack. I realized at that moment that my sympathy for the kid as I lay there in my bag didn't amount to squat. It was Pato Silva, not I, who demonstrated real leadership and care for him.

The guy in the sleeping bag on my other side was the senior enlisted man in the task force, Suboficial Navarrete. Now, I hope this doesn't hurt his feelings too much, because I liked Navarrete and we joked around a lot, but he was the fattest Chilean Marine I ever saw. He was technically and tactically proficient and knew his stuff, and he had somehow even gotten through the commando course at some stage in his life. He was amazingly physically fit for a guy of his size, usually able to hang in there on a run or a hike when some of the skinnier and younger Marines couldn't hold the pace. He was just a big guy and looked terrible in uniform, as if he had ingested an entire other Chilean Marine like an anaconda. He had no trouble keeping up on that day's hike, but in the middle of the night he experienced a serious physical dilemma. About 2 a.m. he was awakened by the urgent need to get out of the bag and go outside the barn and take a leak, but every time he tried to stand up his legs would cramp. He looked over and saw the firewatch[6] over by the barn door with his rifle slung over his shoulder, stamping his feet and rubbing his hands together in a vain attempt to stay warm. Navarrete whispered loudly to the kid, called him over, and told him to help him up. The Marine helped Navarrete up and embraced him momentarily to keep him from toppling over before saying pitifully in singsong Chilean Spanish, "Ah, mi suboficial . . . usted está calientiiiiito."

When we woke up and prepped the boats to go down the Palena River, it was still raining. The fifty-five horsepower engines would spare us the work of paddling the boats down the river, but since all we had to do was sit there on the gunwale tubes, we froze. More than ever, I regretted the foolhardy bravado of not bringing my GORE-TEX as I huddled in my poncho. The scenery of the pristine Aysén region was even more beautiful from the river than from the road. At places, the river was two hundred yards wide, and misty cloudbanks squatted on the low green hills like giant buddhas.

---

6. When the unit is in the field resting for the night, the firewatch is the guard who keeps the fire controlled but still burning, prevents pilferage of military equipment, and provides a minimal early warning system. He usually stands one- or two-hour watches and is relieved by similarly junior Marines.

Figure 8: Freezing in a rubber boat on the Palena River in the south of Chile in 2002.

The boat ride down the fast-flowing river, powered by outboard engines, was rapid, and we soon found ourselves approaching Puerto Marín Balmaceda at the point where the river empties into the Pacific. The rain intensified and we could make out a gray line across the wide river about a mile off our bow. The answer to my question about what the gray line was soon came in the form of hail that pelted us for what seemed like an eternity. It was only pea-sized but hurt like the dickens, and when it finally ended, the bottom of the boat was covered with it. We eventually beached the boats near the port and tried to establish radio contact with the ship while I attempted to walk myself warm up and down the beach. I'd go a few hundred yards up the beach, do about as many push-ups as I could, and walk back and confirm that the radio operators were still trying different antennas and frequencies.

Finally, after establishing communications with the ship and getting the green light to come back aboard, we loaded the boats for the final transit across the open, gray sea back to the *Rancagua*. By the time I climbed back up the wet nets and watched to ensure everyone got back on board, I was closer to hypothermic than I think I've ever been. I went straight to the stateroom I shared with the ship's segundo comandante, stripped out of my wet clothes, and got in my rack under a couple of wool blankets. Barcaza sweet barcaza.

In Charge of the Perros y Gatos

Near the end of my time in Chile in the spring (Chilean fall) of 2002, the entire destacamento headed north to Puerto Aldea for a force-on-force exercise pitting the rifle companies against one another. Force-on-force exercises are a pain in the extreme lower back for the same reason that children playing "army" or "cops and robbers" is chaotic: everyone wants to win and it is often supremely difficult to discern who would have gotten the best of whom in an engagement. Even the US military solution that I used as a young officer,[1] gear that worked by a system of sensors and laser beams, would occasionally be gamed by Marines who achieved exercise immortality by taking the 9V batteries out of their sensor harnesses.

Since we didn't have high-tech gear or even blank ammunition for this exercise, it would be up to controllers like myself, officers accompanying the rifle companies, to determine who, based on positioning of forces, element of surprise, and relative combat power, would have gotten the better of whom in each attack and defense. I had a radio operator with me, but at this point near the end of my two years, having heard many tactical radio conversations, I felt comfortable just taking the handset from him and reporting information the way I would have done in English in the US Marines. Military communications strive for accuracy, clarity, and brevity, and talking on military radio has a few cardinal rules. You never want to hold down the push-to-talk button on the handset for more than about three seconds because enemy direction finders can determine your position and call in artillery or

---

1. Multiple Integrated Laser Engagement System (MILES)

mortars on you. You always want to end a reported element with "over" (*cambio* in Spanish) to signal the operator at the other end that you're ready to receive their transmission so that you don't talk over each other and he doesn't think you've just let up on the push-to-talk switch simply to break up the transmission. To end an entire transmission, you say your call sign and "out." In the movies and on TV, you often hear "over and out," which may have been standard practice in the past, but by the time I was learning to use the radio in the mid '80s all we said was "out." Remember, brevity counts. In Chile, the Marines ended transmissions with the old "over and out" phrase (*cambio y fuera*). And one of the biggest rules is that you never, ever use profanity on the radio.

As soon as we dismounted the trucks at Puerto Aldea, my radio operator and I located the headquarters of the company to whom we were assigned and started walking with them as the company fanned out and moved tactically into the low hills. The missions assigned to the companies were designed to make them fight each other in varying scenarios and on different terrain. One company would be assigned to defend a hilltop or road junction and an adjacent company would be given the mission to attack and secure it. Much of my work consisted of walking in the dark with all the gear I would need for three or four days in the field, while trying not to stumble on rocks, limbs, and low-lying bushes. In a low-tech environment in which few troops are equipped with night vision devices, darkness is the infantryman's friend. To move around unseen is to be more survivable, and for that same reason, we stayed off the roads when the probability of contact with the enemy was high. So you move slowly, feeling around with your shins and gently moving brush out of the way with your hands while trying to maintain visual contact with the man in front of you. You want to be close enough to see him, but not too close, since survivability as an infantryman is linked to dispersion. The more dispersed your unit is, the fewer people killed by one mine or IED,[2] one grenade or mortar, or one burst of automatic weapons fire. Poorly trained, tired, or sloppy Marines will bunch up, both on the march and at halts. The Chilean Marines even have a word to describe poor tactical

---

2. Improvised Explosive Device

dispersion: *achoclonado. Choclo* is Chilean Spanish for "corn" and the invented Chilean verb *achoclonarse* means to be bunched tightly together like kernels of corn on the cob.

Over time, you can tell one man from another by their outlines in the darkness and the way they wear their gear. In the moonlight I could easily spot the company commander I accompanied, Teniente Guevara, because he was more robust than most everyone else and he routed his chinstrap up over the front of his helmet. As the night wears on and you get sleepy and bored, the task of staying tactical and focused becomes exceedingly tedious. At Ranger School, we would sometimes patrol for days on end in a constant state of sleep deprivation. I recall occasionally inhabiting a dark netherworld of consciousness on patrol, like a twist on the Schrödinger's cat thought experiment, being simultaneously awake and asleep staggering along with a rifle in my hand. Sometimes in my life as an infantryman I would have to walk all night, struggling to stay awake and focused while silently shifting pack straps from one place on aching shoulders to another to do so, but thankfully the training area at Puerto Aldea was small enough for us to move from one mission to another in a few hours.

One factor that complicated stealthy movement was the abundance of pheasants. Puerto Aldea would be a Disneyland for pheasant hunters, and Chileans did hunt them, but the population of wild pheasant, often described as *plaga* (plague), thrived in an abundance that stayed far ahead of its predators. You would be quietly moving through the brush scanning the skyline for sign of the enemy and suddenly be scared out of your wits by an explosion of feathers and flapping wings as those enormous game birds loudly spooked into flight under your feet (and goodbye, tactical silence). The pheasant explosion happened to me two or three times at Puerto Aldea, and each time it would take a half hour for my heart rate to go back down to normal.

If I knew we were going to be in one place at night for long, I'd stretch out under my poncho liner, one of the greatest military products of all time. As the name implies, the poncho liner was made to complement the more-or-less rainproof poncho by tying little sewn-in strings to the grommets along the edges of the poncho. But the liner itself, feather-light, compact, and insulated, did a pretty good job of keeping you warm at night down to about forty-five degrees if you were out of the wind. I'd tuck the poncho liner around my legs and torso like a blanket and lie back on my pack and look up at the stars. I had one of those handheld PDAs (personal data assistant) that were big back before cell phones could do everything. It had an astronomy application on it that I used to identify the constellations in the Chilean night sky. Chile is lightly populated and remarkably free of light pollution, which is one reason why some of the most important observatories in the world are located in northern Chile. Most nights the skies were stunningly beautiful, with the Southern Cross being the focus of navigation instead of the North Star. Orion was, to me, always the centerpiece of the Chilean sky, the figure I looked for first. The three large stars that make up his belt were known in Chile as *Las tres Marías.*

The second night of the force-on-force the company I accompanied attacked an adjacent rifle company, and when the lines crossed, words were exchanged that resulted in a physical confrontation between a sergeant from the defending unit and a private from the attacking one. Now, Chileans, even Chilean Marines, are peaceful people, generally speaking. The homicide rate per 100,000 people in Chile, year in and year out, is about half of what it is in the United States. I once saw an incident of "road rage" near the Reñaca Beach in Viña in which two Chileans exited their cars at an intersection shouting at each other. They came at each other enraged, with fists raised, but neither landed a punch and within a minute they affectionately embraced, got back into their cars, and calmly drove away under the nonplussed gaze of me and about a dozen Chileans. Anyway, in this clash between the two rifle companies, the Chilean Marine equivalent of, "I shot you"—"No way, I shot you first," devolved into the sergeant launching a vigorous kick into the backside of the private, which I included in my customary report of the engagement via radio. I hesitated mid-report, though, because I wasn't sure if *culo* counted as profanity. My understanding of what was and wasn't profanity in Chile was hampered by the fact that I spent most of my waking hours with Chilean Marines and Navy guys where profanity is the lingua franca.

The point of my uncertainty about Chilean profanity was the fact that the Chilean bad words were not simply Spanish translations of English bad words. In fact, when I was initially getting my bearings in Chile and starting to understand what was being said, I thought, "Oh, this is remarkable. These guys don't use profanity," which was totally wrong. It turns out that many Chileans use profanity with the same passion and artistry with which Michelangelo wielded a chisel. There are many wondrous obscenities in Chilean Spanish, but the preferred *palabrota* is written as *güevón*, *huevón*, or *weón*. Despite the efforts of some Chileans to invent polite narratives about the etymology of the word, *huevón* is related to *huevo* (egg), a euphemism for testicle.[3] The Spanish augmentative "-ón" or "-ona" expresses the idea of a "big old" something. But the huevón is not so named due to having "big balls" in the English sense of the phrase; instead it refers to a man who has been rendered permanently useless by an untreated inguinal hernia. *Huevón* has come to be the Swiss Army knife of Chilean profanity, with the infinitive *huevear* being the point of origin from which spring many derivations, including an adjective version and incredibly, a physiologically impossible feminine *huevona* reserved for females whose ignominy earns them that title. You would ask heatedly, "¿Tengo cara de huevón?" to ask, "Do I look stupid to you?" One of my favorites was the phrase *huevón telescópico*, which implied that someone was such a profound huevón that it was evident from long distance.

In most contexts, *huevón* is a supremely offensive word, equivalent to our "f-word." But it can be applied in a friendly, intimate way, especially if you pronounced it sloppily, without the "v." The standard greeting I would hear among male friends was, "¿Cómo estai, hue'ón?" So, "hue'ón" turns out to be used almost exactly like "man" in English. I knew the commandant of the Chilean Marine Corps, Admiral Gastón Arriagada, truly liked me when he casually called me "hue'ón" in a conversation. So when I was reporting the butt-kicking incident on the radio, I caught myself just before I said *culo* (more or less "ass" in English) and opted for *trasero* (basically "behind") in Spanish, which I was told elicited a lot of laughter in the command post and became part of the narrative that followed me around the Chilean Marine Corps for a time after. With characteristic exaggeration, Chileans would tell

---

3. Never ask a waiter in a Spanish-speaking restaurant if he has *huevos*. Ask instead, "¿Hay huevos?" (Are there eggs?).

the story saying *trasero* with a gringo accent, which is a lie. My grammar is not perfect, but I know how to say my "r's" in Spanish.

Attacking and defending with three companies rotating through different stations left us with an odd number. I don't think we had thought through how to provide an aggressor force for the third company, and I recommended that we put together a provisional unit, a "Dogs and Cats Company" I called it, out of the headquarters company. As soon as the recommendation came out of my mouth, I wished I had used a different phrase. I was learning the hard way to be careful of sounding scornful or contemptuous of anything Chilean. Marines anywhere in the world deal with challenges in the field with complaints, sarcastic remarks, and gallows humor, and I, after nearly two years with them, thought of the destacamento as our unit, our situation, our equipment, etc. As a foreigner, though, I never totally had the right to complain except among close friends. Many Chileans had a vision of the United States as a place where everything worked well, where everything was organized, and where everything was the best. So, many of them resented me joking around or describing Chilean things in negative or derogatory terms because they thought I came from a Marine Corps (and country) where everything functioned perfectly. But in this case the Chileans liked the suggestion and besides, the phrase *perros y gatos* fit right in with the Chilean linguistic custom of animalizing so many situations. In Chile, a guy is a *gallo*, or "rooster." Children are *cabros chicos* (precisely, "little kids"). To have a good time is to *pasarlo chancho* (which I take to mean "have as much fun as pigs do"). One of my all-time favorite Chilean animal expressions is the puzzling *quedar como chaleco de mono* ("to be like a monkey's vest"). Some explanation: think of the little monkey that accompanies the organ grinder. The little vest he wears is bound to be ill-fitting, given the "one-size-fits-all" nature of dressing small monkeys and the need for the poor organ grinder to economize. So the phrase *quedó como chaleco de mono* would be applied to someone who was humiliated and wound up looking bad.

Nearly all the Marines in the Headquarters and Service company are specialists: radio operators, repairmen, and even cooks and bakers. But one of the real strengths of any Marine unit is the ethos of "every Marine a rifleman," which ensures that even the specialists are trained to fight. We hastily organized the headquarters Marines into a small rifle company and marched off through the thorny shrubs (*espinos*) to "fight" the third company in the Batallón de Fusileros, where the perros and gatos distinguished themselves by their solid tactical performance and seemed to thoroughly enjoy the chance to do something tactical outside of their narrow specialties. By the time the exercise ended in the late morning of the fourth day, my radio operator and I found ourselves walking back to the headquarters tired, footsore, dirty, and starving after four days of busy field time. It was rare that we carried combat rations in the field in the Chilean Marines. The famous Meals, Ready to Eat (MREs) that we typically ate in the field in the US Marines were expensive, so we usually ate meals provided by the field kitchen at the headquarters. The problem was that if the tactical situation required the headquarters to move, everyone would be missing at least one meal. We each carried a small tin plate and spoon (the entire issued mess kit was too heavy and noisy), and a trick I learned from Francisco Fierro was to bring along some thin plastic bags. When we were served a meal, I'd put a small plastic bag over my plate, place the food on top, eat, and then turn the bag clean side out and tie a little knot in it. Voilà! No cleanup. I always thought the food in the field was good, even though Chilean Marines complained about it[4] exactly like US Marines complain about Marine chow. By the time my radio operator and I got back to the headquarters, much of the field kitchen had been packed up and moved, but some hot food was still available in one of the marmite cans.[5] We heaped up plates of some unidentifiable casserole, sat down on ammo cans, and dined as content as dukes.

---

4. Whenever we were served fricassee, the Chilean Marines would call it *fracasé*, which means "I failed."

5. Marmite cans were insulated food containers painted green.

Far from the Flagpole

In the Marine Corps we would sometimes refer to proximity to the headquarters, either geographically or in terms of how often they thought about you, as being close to or far from the flagpole. At 1st Reconnaissance Battalion in the late '80s, we were considered far from the flagpole since our higher headquarters, that of 1st Marine Division, was clear on the other side of Camp Pendleton, about an hour's drive away. The good news was that we were largely free from frequent visits from the commanding general and his staff, but we also risked being forgotten when it came time to assign resources. The phrase also came to be applied to how much you as an individual were remembered or forgotten, how much your work was viewed and valued, and how much of it went unseen, factors that could be supremely important when it came to selection for promotion, top-level school, or taking command. Any assignment outside of the conventional US Marine Corps was away from the flagpole, but Chile was about as far away, in every sense, as it could possibly be.

I tried to keep myself on the radar screen at US Marine Corps headquarters by e-mailing unofficial situation reports to the office that had overall responsibility for me. Normally, deployed units send periodic situation reports (called SITREPs) back to their higher headquarters to advise them on their past and near future activities, stocks of supplies, and pending requests. Mine was similarly formatted but centered on my activities with the destacamento. I kept all the information totally unclassified since I was sending it out in the clear via e-mail. I thought it was important that headquarters remember that I was with an operational Marine unit, albeit one from another country, often deploying aboard ship and going to the field and getting applied field experience, not sitting in the embassy in Santiago dimpling my knees with teacups. I would do my best never to nitpick what I thought were short-comings of my Chilean hosts for two reasons: first, it sure wouldn't make me look any better to be part of a messed-up unit. Second, I always assumed that the Chilean intelligence agents at some level were reading my e-mails, and I saw no value in antagonizing the people I worked with every day. After I had been there a few months, I heard about a Chilean Navy officer who had been outed as gay because Chilean Naval intelligence was reading his e-mails. He was married with a couple of kids and was exchanging e-mails with his lover on the desktop computer in his apartment, which was only a couple of blocks from my house. "It read just like a guy and a girl," a Chilean officer told me in a scandalized whisper. The Chilean Navy intercepted it, and he was out of the service within twenty-four hours. I immediately figured that if they were reading his, they were reading mine. Chilean Naval intelligence was active, but ham-handed. After I left Chile, I read about a couple of Chilean agents who were caught bumbling around late at night in an Argentine liaison office in Punta Arenas in an episode that seemed like something out of a Pink Panther movie.

The fact that I got promoted to lieutenant colonel in 2001 was a good sign that the big Green Rifle Club back in the States had not forgotten me. Later that same year, I got more good news: I appeared as an alternate on the list for command selection, which is great for the first year of eligibility. Command as a Lieutenant Colonel would be at the battalion level,[1] which to me was (and is) the greatest thing you could ever get to do in the Corps. I remember standing watch in the battalion command post as a young lieutenant, which always meant long hours of boredom and making rounds, studying the photos of former battalion commanders in 8x10 frames that were hung with millimetric precision in chronological order along the wall outside the commander's office. It seemed to me that being a battalion commander gave you a foothold in history, a certain amount of Marine Corps immortality, albeit in the form of a grim photo in a cheap frame.

---

1. Battalions consist of between 800 and 1,200 Marines, depending on the type of unit.

When I finally got in contact with my monitor on the phone, he said he had never received my e-mail volunteering for assignment to a unit going to Afghanistan. He was also surprised to realize it was time for me to move and had planned to leave me in Chile for another year. When I reminded him that the job was supposed to be a two-year assignment, he told me he wanted to send me to SOUTHCOM in Miami because I had experience in Latin America and spoke Spanish and Portuguese.[2] Since the job would maintain my contact with Latin America, it sounded good, so I didn't argue. You don't have to agree with where the monitor wants to send you, but they will generally try to avoid sending officers to assignments kicking and screaming. What he didn't mention was that since I was going to a joint assignment, I would be ineligible for command selection for two years.[3] I found that out later. During my time serving at SOUTHCOM, nearly the whole Marine Corps went to war in Afghanistan and Iraq. There was no way I was going to be favorably compared with a guy who had spent a year in Iraq. To be a Latin American expert in the US Marine Corps after 2001 turned into something akin to being an accomplished ice hockey player in Haiti, and that appearance as an alternate on the command selection list in my first year of eligibility was as close as I ever got.

Our last few weeks in Chile were a whirlwind of goodbyes, official and unofficial. The boys' classes had parties for them since they were leaving in the middle of the school year. The tennis ladies had a couple of events for Margaret. She presented the tennis clubhouse with an old refinished racquet with a small engraved plaque on it. The destacamento had a nice departure ceremony where they gave me a beautiful pair of Chilean huaso spurs in a glass case. In return I gave the cámara de oficiales a dartboard in a nice wooden case with a little plaque engraved with my name and dates of service with the unit. The officers had a barbecue for our whole family, and one night the subtenientes, the young officers, dragged me through

---

2. I had been studying Portuguese to take the Defense Language Proficiency Test and to be eligible for more language pay. The test was geared toward reading and listening comprehension, so that's what I studied for. In truth, I could speak very little, and now that I teach elementary Italian, I avoid speaking and hearing Portuguese at all costs.

3. The military services receive an adverse report on their commitment to "jointness" if they pull people out of joint assignments before they serve for three years.

half the bars in Valparaíso. Although the Chilean Marines were incredibly thoughtful in the elaborate *despedidas* (send-offs, goodbyes) they had for us, the ceremonies were more a function of how Chileans are than how well regarded I was. They just seemed to be the world champions of ceremonies and commemorations even when they seemed to gain nothing directly from them. Near the end of every year when the conscripts' mandatory service ended, we would have a despedida for them, a little wine and empanada, and then when it was time for them to leave, we lined the road out to the main gate and sang the Chilean Marine Hymn while they marched out for the last time in civilian clothes. Being a conscript in the Chilean Marines is no picnic, and I would say that, to a man, they looked forward to getting on with their post-conscription lives, but several of them openly wept as they marched to the gate singing the hymn with us for the last time. The commemorations were not even limited to departures of people but were also employed for the arrivals of things. When the Chilean Marine Corps purchased a dozen used trucks from the Italian military, we had a ceremony to mark the incorporation of the trucks in the unit's rolling stock. The desta-camento formed on the parade ground to hear a reading of the history of how the trucks were acquired, what their capabilities were, and how those capabilities contributed to the combat power of the unit. A priest even blessed the trucks with prayer and sprinkling of holy water. Something like this would have been considered a waste of time in the US Marines, but I could tell that the Chilean Marines were prouder of those trucks and took better care of them because of that ceremony.

When it came time for the move, our household goods were packed up, we cleaned the house, and we called the real estate agency to have them come inspect the house and return our security deposit. We went through an eight-page checklist as we walked around the house with a representa-tive from Silvia's office. We were given a thumbs-up from her and were promised that we would soon receive our security deposit. Despite visits to Silvia's house, phone calls, and written correspondence, we never saw a dime of our money, some three thousand dollars. Clearly, we were getting jammed because we were foreigners and they knew that if they could just avoid us for a few more days, we'd be back in the States where we couldn't do anything. I was afraid that if I made too much noise about it, it would make things tough for the guy who came with his family to replace me.

Our last couple of days in Chile, we stayed in a cabin on a beautiful section of rocky beach owned by the Navy. It was bittersweet to leave friends and a country we had grown to love, but we were enthusiastic about being closer to family back in the States, back in a place where everything felt more familiar and simpler. As we waited to board the plane in Santiago for the flight to Miami, our older son JD had a short conversation in Spanish with the man sitting next to him about soccer while we were watching one of the 2002 World Cup matches. I was moved by this simple act: my nine-year-old son being confident enough to engage in conversation in Spanish with an adult stranger about a game we in the US still don't understand. At that moment, I felt like we had come a long, long way from the house fire. My heart was full.

So, since we had made so many great friends in Chile and had such a great experience overall, did it ever cross my mind to make plans to come back and settle down in Chile after my Marine Corps career? Sure. We considered it even though we didn't know when that would be. But I was a little leery of the possibility because of what happened to a retired US Navy officer who had the house of his dreams built down in Puerto Montt. Soon after he moved in, a fish processing plant was built nearby that generated a stench that made the place unlivable. He had no legal recourse, and he and his wife wound up moving back to the US. When the monitor said he hadn't planned to move me at the two-year mark, I was tempted to stay for another year. But I felt like I had to get closer to the flagpole (although a joint assignment in Miami was not exactly close) and back to the US. The feeling of being a foreigner is a strong thing, and I knew that although I liked Chile a great deal, it wasn't our long-term home. Plus, the fact that our country was sending a ton of troops to Afghanistan, Iraq, and other parts of southwest Asia made me feel a pull to get back to the States. We always felt a little out of place—well-liked, but regarded always as interlopers. The stealing of our security deposit was another reminder that in any kind of argument between me and a Chilean, as a foreigner I would invariably get the short end of the stick.

We moved to Kendall, an immigrant-heavy, middle-class part of Miami, where we rented a nice house from an elderly Lebanese couple whose primary mode of conversation with us and each other was yelling. I thought that living in Kendall would be a great place to maintain my Spanish language skills, but it turned that nearly everyone was bilingual. In the checkout line at a grocery store or Lowe's, the cashier would wait on the three people in front of me in Spanish, then look at me and ask me in English, "Hi, how are you today? Did you find everything you were looking for?" Sometimes when I did try to speak Spanish with a Latino in Miami, I was met with a stony coldness that taught me that language choice is not just linguistic but sometimes political and often deeply personal and intimate. I can count on one hand the number of times it was totally appropriate for me to speak Spanish in three-and-a-half years out in the general population in and around Miami. This was disappointing, but I had plenty of chances to speak Spanish at work.

When I started working at SOUTHCOM, I was frustrated by how dismissive a lot of people were about my Chile assignment, as if I had been on vacation for the previous two years. One Army colonel asked me if I was ready to finally get to work. When I worked in Miami, only a small percentage of the people assigned to SOUTHCOM had ever lived and worked with Latin American militaries, and they carried their prejudices about US superiority into their attitudes at the job. I was assigned to the Commander's Action Group, a part of the four-star general's personal staff. There were four of us, one from each service, with an Army colonel in charge, and we worked long hours together in a big, hectic cubicle. We wrote speeches, did research, and helped plan the commander's travel and meetings with international dignitaries. Most of the people assigned to the Commander's Action Group were handpicked by their services. They were whip-smart, and smart people tend to be funny, so we had a good time in that cubicle. And we all spoke Spanish.

I found myself occasionally trying to offer alternative points of view on US policy proposals that I knew would be viewed as strong-armed and unfair by Latin American militaries. Here's a prime example: The International Criminal Court was established in 2002 to prosecute crimes that national judiciaries will not prosecute. The US, after initially showing interest in joining the ICC, refused to ratify membership along with several other countries. Obviously, some prime candidates for prosecution by the ICC would have been the intellectual authors of the detention center at Guantánamo Bay, which would include members of the Bush cabinet and administration, right on down to my boss as the commander of SOUTHCOM.[4] Soon after, the US Congress passed the American Serviceman's Protection Act (ASPA), which prohibited selling military aid to countries who had ratified the treaty establishing the ICC (just about every country in Latin America). Military aid included people from those countries coming to the US for training and bilateral training between our armed forces and theirs. Countries who were ICC members could get around the prohibition by signing an agreement to not hand over each other's citizens to the ICC, a provision known as Article 98. ASPA, which I believe was written without any concern whatsoever for people in uniform, seemed to assume that the militaries from other countries would be so desperate for training and equipment from the US that they'd be willing to be bullied into an agreement with the US that might not square with their countries' interests. And I knew for certain that the Chileans didn't see the US as the only game in town. They were being courted heavily by the Chinese when I was there.[5] When I pointed this out, my loyalty was called into question by the chief of staff of US Marine Forces South. I argued that I was highlighting the negative consequences of this policy precisely because I had seen the costs of disengaging in terms of losing US contact and influence. But he was employing the go-to technique for chicken hawks during the Bush administration. If you're not totally on board with every policy decision, you're called unpatriotic.

My point of view was eventually validated a few months before I retired by my last boss at SOUTHCOM, General Bantz Craddock, who testified before the House Armed Services Committee in 2005 that ASPA was creating a vacuum of US engagement in Latin America that would be filled by other partners.

---

4. Guantánamo Bay fell under SOUTHCOM's administrative and operational control since it's in the Caribbean.

5. One of the few events at the destacamento I was asked not to be present for was a visit by a Chinese delegation that included seven admirals and generals.

Epilogue

When Margaret and I returned for a short visit in 2018, we found Chile dealing with the same changes that are affecting much of the rest of the world. The formerly homogenous population was now leavened with immigrants from Haiti, Venezuela, and Colombia, prompting Francisco and me to play a curious game of "guess where the immigrant is from" whenever we went out in Santiago. After listening one day to the short interchange between Francisco and the young man working the counter at a pizza place, I asked the guy if he was from Medellin, Colombia. He said, "No, Cali" (I had erred by 205 miles). Francisco asked our waiter at another restaurant if he was from Venezuela. He answered, "Sí, de lo que queda" (Yes, from what's left of it). In visual terms, the most impactful demographic change is the marked increase of black people in Chile, prompting nativist conjecture about what being Chilean means and looks like. I wonder if that attitude will change if some day, some son of Haitian immigrants scores the goal that helps Chile qualify for the World Cup or win a South American tournament.

The earthquake tremors that have shaken Chile since before it was Chile have reminded the people there of their tenuous peace with nature, and now concerns about severe drought and disappearing ice fields in the south are increasing. Rising sea levels have breached the seawall at Viña del Mar and flooded some of what used to be the most valuable downtown apartments. The coast road between Viña and Concón was always generally free of big buildings and provided an uninterrupted view of the ocean, but by 2018 at least twenty new high-rise apartment buildings had been built along the beach side of the road, putting thousands of additional vehicles into the mix of local traffic. Whether the increased fear of criminality was justified or inflated by political rhetoric and the twenty-four-hour news cycle, our friends' preoccupation with threats to their safety and property was strong, constant, and all too real. We made the trip suspecting that the Chile we last experienced in 2002 was long gone, a warm, nostalgic memory. We were surprised to discover that it no longer existed for our Chilean friends, either.

Figure 9: Margaret, Mark, John David, and Jackson McGraw at Viña del Mar, Chile, in 2002.

Chile was not just where we were happy, but the place in time where the rich green fields of our futures expanded invitingly before us, before we and our Chilean friends had become the meat in a worry sandwich of constant concern about parents in their eighties and children in their twenties. Most of us had, in one way or another, suffered tremendous heartbreak and family crises in the intervening years. For many of us, our kids, who had seemed like perfect blank slates that our love and careful parenting were preparing for success and happiness, had run headlong into the challenges and dys-functionality of a world whipsawed by social media and an economic system increasingly geared to benefit the very few.

Some of our Chilean Navy friends were still on active duty. Many others were retired but still worked full-time with the Navy in some capacity. Some exceptions were Hugo Huerta, the famous Peanut head, who went back to school, got certified as a psychologist, and has a practice as a psychotherapist in Valparaíso. Walter Matthews parlayed his Marine skills into a business doing survival training for civilians. Francisco Fierro, after working security for a casino for a while, shifted to coordinating security for several warehouses throughout Chile for an international ship-ping company.

Our trip back to Chile didn't include going by and visiting my old destacamento. It was July, right in the middle of their training calendar, and I felt like I would be intruding. I'm sure I know a couple of guys there, but I hadn't planned anything with them and I hadn't been invited. Institutions move on and individuals become faint footnotes if they are remembered at all. Because we didn't go by the destacamento and the tennis clubhouse at the Club Naval de Campo was closed when we had dinner there, we didn't get to see if the dartboard and plaque I left the destacamento or the repurposed antique tennis racquet/plaque Margaret gave to the tennis club were still on display in the cámara de oficiales and the clubhouse. I suppose they are not. I imagine they are in a landfill somewhere. I am completely at peace with either possibility.

Dante Alighieri finished writing *Divine Comedy* the year before his death at age fifty-six. Miguel de Cervantes started writing *Don Quixote* while he was in prison at fifty years old and finished the second tome of the novel the year before his death in 1616.[1] I write this similarly on the back nine of life and several years removed from our Chile experience from 2000–2002. It could be that people in their fifties begin to look backward and feel compelled to tell their stories because of the fear that tonight or tomorrow morning a stroke or heart attack or early Alzheimer's may deprive them of their ability to tell it. I think I have felt the same compulsion even though I plan to live another forty years or so. Since I haven't been exiled and threatened with execution like Dante and I didn't write this at a time when the Inquisition was still burning people at the stake in Toledo like when Cervantes was writing, I felt no need to encode what I experienced in terza rima or fiction.

I have checked with some of my Chilean friends to confirm names and places and times, but I readily concede that what I have written has been run through the laundry of my sentimental memory, now tinged by the passage of over seventeen years. I had no ax to grind with anyone as I wrote this. In fact, my feelings of gratitude for the people and the experiences filled my heart to overflowing as I recalled all we went through in Chile. I have tried my best to avoid making myself look good, but I have also omitted some of the most colossally foolish things that I did.

Our two-year stay in Chile was the keystone experience of our family life, and it changed the way I see the world. It convinced me more than ever of the spark of the divine that exists in the most humble and unassuming person. It taught me that despite the significant differences of language and culture, there is an overwhelmingly greater humanity that unites us. I came away with a better understanding of the power of ceremony and commemoration, the strength of personal relationships, and the gift of time spent together. As soon as we could, Margaret and I pursued work that gave us time to enjoy our lives together, and we started to put more of our money into experiences and less into things. We resolved that when we got back to the US, we'd return the favor of hospitality that the Chileans had shown us, to be a bridge of welcome to international visitors, especially if they speak Spanish.

We knew that, although we were welcome as visitors in Chile, the place was not made or designed for us long-term. I understood and accepted that

---

1. Although these are works of fiction, they contain many experiences and episodes from the writers' lives.

fact, which made me more carefully consider my place in my own country. When I got back to the States, the scales fell from my eyes and I realized that my nation, however pluralistic our best national narrative may be, was designed by people like me for the comfort and benefit of people like me, and that, although I had to serve and work hard and take risks, the wind had always been at my back. So, I resolved to do my best to never let any of my fellow citizens feel like they were visitors in their own country, deprived of equal rights, standing, or voice.

Our Chile experience has made me cherish and value some of the things that are truly great about the United States, the creativity and freedom and opportunity to achieve just about anything you're willing to work hard enough for. And I've been given a great gift of seeing my own culture from a distance through the eyes of others, to question and not just blindly accept that our way is the only or best way.

About the Author

Mark McGraw was born in Fort Worth, Texas, grew up in Alexandria, Louisiana, and lived and worked in thirty-four countries during his twenty years of service as a US Marine officer. He is a writer, translator, and language professor, having earned a master's degree in Modern Languages and a PhD in Hispanic Studies from Texas A&M University. He has also translated Joseph Avski's *Heart of Scorpio* (Tiny Toe Press, 2012) and *One Step from Juarez* (Mouthfeel Press, 2015).